New Short Plays: 3

HOWARD BARKER
  Cheek

JOHN GRILLO
  Number Three

DON HAWORTH
  There's No Point
  In Arguing The Toss

PIP SIMMONS
  Superman

These plays were first published in Great Britain in 1972
by Eyre Methuen Ltd
11 New Fetter Lane London EC4P 4EE
Set by Expression Printers Ltd
Printed in Great Britain by
The Redwood Press, Trowbridge, Wiltshire

SBN 413 28860 9 Hardback
    413 28870 6 Paperback

Methuen Playscripts

The Methuen Playscripts series exists
to extend the range of plays in print by
publishing work which is not yet widely
known but which has already earned a
place in the repertoire of the modern
theatre.

New Short Plays: 3

The past few years have seen a revival of interest in the
short play. This third Methuen Playscript collection of
plays by four British writers reflects something of the
range of modern writing for the theatre within the short
play form.

CHEEK by Howard Barker, a wry, compassionate study
of a 'drop-out', was first presented at the Royal Court's
Theatre Upstairs in 1970.

NUMBER THREE by John Grillo portrays a savagely
hilarious battle of wits and wills between a lunatic and
a male nurse: originally directed by Frederick Proud
at the Soho Theatre Club in 1970.

THERE'S NO POINT IN ARGUING THE TOSS by Don
Haworth is a funny and poignant radio play, first broadcast in 1967.

SUPERMAN, the Pip Simmons Theatre Group's show, is
based on the American comic strip cartoon and has been
widely performed in Britain and Europe.

Other Methuen Playscripts

Paul Ableman	TESTS
	BLUE COMEDY
Barry Bermange	NATHAN AND TABILETH
	and OLDENBURG
John Bowen	THE CORSICAN BROTHERS
Howard Brenton	REVENGE
	CHRISTIE IN LOVE and other plays
Henry Chapman	YOU WON'T ALWAYS BE ON TOP
Peter Cheeseman	THE KNOTTY
David Cregan	THREE MEN FOR COLVERTON
	TRANSCENDING and THE DANCERS
	THE HOUSES BY THE GREEN
	MINIATURES
Rosalyn Drexler	THE INVESTIGATION and HOT
	BUTTERED ROLL
Simon Gray	THE IDIOT
Harrison, Melfi,	NEW SHORT PLAYS
Howard	
Duffy, Harrison,	NEW SHORT PLAYS: 2
Owens	
Henry Livings	GOOD GRIEF!
	THE LITTLE MRS FOSTER SHOW
	HONOUR AND OFFER
	PONGO PLAYS 1-6
John McGrath	EVENTS WHILE GUARDING THE
	BOFORS GUN
David Mercer	THE GOVERNOR'S LADY
Georges Michel	THE SUNDAY WALK
Rodney Milgate	A REFINED LOOK AT EXISTENCE
Guillaume Oyono–	THREE SUITORS: ONE HUSBAND
Mbia	and UNTIL FURTHER NOTICE
Alan Plater	CLOSE THE COALHOUSE DOOR
David Selbourne	THE PLAY OF WILLIAM COOPER
	AND EDMUND DEW–NEVETT
	THE TWO BACKED BEAST
	DORABELLA
Johnny Speight	IF THERE WEREN'T ANY BLACKS
	YOU'D HAVE TO INVENT THEM
Martin Sperr	TALES FROM LANDSHUT
Boris Vian	THE KNACKER'S ABC
Lanford Wilson	HOME FREE! and THE MADNESS
	OF LADY BRIGHT

CONTENTS

HOWARD BARKER
Cheek

JOHN GRILLO
Number Three

DON HAWORTH
There's No Point in Arguing the Toss

PIP SIMMONS THEATRE GROUP
Superman

Cheek

Howard Barker

Cheek was first presented at the Theatre Upstairs on September 11, 1971, with the following cast:

LAURIE, an unemployed 20-year-old	Tom Chadbon
BILL, a similar friend	Ken Cranham
MUM, Laurie's mother, about 45	Diane Hart
DAD, her husband, about 50	Richard Butler
SHIRLEY, a neighbour, about 20	Susan Littler
JANICE) girls out for an evening	Liz Edmiston
ADELE)	Cheryl Hall
A SCHOOLGIRL	Liz Edmiston
AN AMERICAN OFFICER	Marshall Jones
A WOMAN OF 35	

(The part of A WOMAN OF 35 was omitted from this production.)

Directed by William Gaskill
Designed by Di Seymour

Act One

SCENE ONE

A domestic interior, not overburdened with props. For example, two soft chairs, a table, a TV set, a mirror. This should not occupy the whole stage, but leave an area in darkness where a spotlight can isolate actors outside the main action.

LAURIE and BILL are sprawled in the chairs. It is important that LAURIE never sits, only sprawls. A long pause to establish the reigning atmosphere of boredom.

LAURIE: You know what I want?

(Pause.)

Go on, guess what I want?

(Pause. BILL gets out a packet of cigarettes, takes one, throws the packet to LAURIE.)

BILL: I know what you want.

(Pause.)

LAURIE: I'm under a compulsion.

(Pause.)

An imperative urge, you might say.

(Pause.)

BILL: It has been a long time.

LAURIE: Oh, an eternity, a bloody millennium.

BILL: I'm not bothered myself. Not that eager.

(Pause.)

Of course, I have been ill.

LAURIE: Oh, you have. You have been ill. It's sapped your strength. It's drained your tiny little impulse...

BILL: You think it'll come back, do you?

LAURIE: Who can tell?

BILL: You don't think it's eaten away at all them hundreds of yards of tiny little tubes, do you?

LAURIE: You wait till we're hanging about outside them school gates, our eyes glazed, rivetted on those tight little bums in their flimsy little knickers... it'll come back.

BILL (leaning back, inhaling deeply): You have a way with words...

(Pause.)

LAURIE: You know, I could have a lasting, deep, meaningful affair with one of them little whores... get my hands round them firm little buttocks... I'm going to, you know... I'm not passing my twenty-third birthday before I've had one...

BILL: I like to see a man with an aim in life...

SCENE TWO

Lights out on set.

A SCHOOLGIRL is spotlighted in the blank area of the stage. She is in a penitent posture, hands behind back, head bent. LAURIE, in a teacher's gown and clasping a ruler, appears beside her.

LAURIE: I didn't want to have to do this, Sylvia. You drove me to it. I don't approve of corporal punishment, as a matter of fact, but there are times when even I have to resort to it.

(SYLVIA bends double, her backside in the air. LAURIE climbs
onto her back.

Lights out.)

SCENE THREE

Action continues from Scene One.

BILL: I think the news is on...

LAURIE: News?

BILL: You switch it on, you're nearest.

LAURIE (reaching for the switch): You worry me, do you know that?
You're a cause for concern. You'd rather watch Gordon Honeycombe's glossy bonce than talk about schoolgirls. That's unhealthy.

(LAURIE assumes a CBS accent): In the Vietnam conflict a US
General has pleaded guilty to a charge of raping three hundred
virgins in one week. I was under the impression it was part of the
pacification campaign, he said...

(Pause. BILL doesn't laugh.)

BILL: It's not loud enough...

LAURIE: It has to get worked up...

BILL: I can't hear it!

LAURIE: Look, I'm not letting Gordon Honeycombe afflict my father
in his final moments. I'm allowed to spill his medicine down his
chin, but you're not. I can pull his pyjama cord too tight, but not
you. It's my privilege, you see?

(BILL shrugs. Pause.)

BILL: I've never seen a dying man. I haven't. In all my life I've never
seen a dying man. Not a corpse either.

LAURIE: Be my guest.

BILL: I might catch something.

LAURIE: You would, wouldn't you? I expect –

BILL: Shut up, it's the Royal Tour.

LAURIE: Oh, I'm very interested in the Royal Tour, I am. Especially the Duke's tour of the Queen.

BILL: You could be arrested for saying that.

LAURIE: I have the most disgusting mind. I shock myself sometimes.

(Pause.)

BILL (sudden recall): Here, did you finish that door to door survey?

LAURIE (switching off the set): Now there...

(He goes to a drawer in the table.)

I've made definite progress.

(He reads from a foolscap sheet.)

First question. Do you have all three television channels? Second. Which do you view most frequently? Three. What is your favourite programme? And so on. I don't waste my time, you see. I've got thirty questions here, and some of them need long answers.

BILL: Yeah, but what if the talent's no good, you don't want to -

LAURIE: I've made provision! It's all right. If she's hopeless, there's a special top sheet which takes about two minutes. The other one takes a minimum of twenty, which should get you as far as the sitting room. After that - you're on your own, and may the best man win.

BILL (perusing the document): This is all good stuff... what do you reckon on our chances?

LAURIE (sitting): On these new estates, there are only two kinds of women. Neurotics and nymphos. Well, some are both of course. Three kinds, if you like. They're probably the most pissed-off women on earth. Bored, neglected, frustrated, over-sexed, and under-shagged. There are hundreds of them within a few acres, and they are literally dying for a ring on the two-tone doorbell.

BILL: What if they ask for an identity card?

LAURIE: What nympho ever asked for an identity card?

BILL: Sounds too easy...

LAURIE: It is too easy. Straight in the door, straight up the nylon worsted stair carpet and flat out on the Slumberland spring interior. What could be easier than that?

BILL: There's got to be a catch somewhere... everyone would do it...

LAURIE: Yeah, but they haven't got the nerve, have they? It's like everything else, you have to go that bit further than everybody else. We have to be beyond the run of common men.

BILL: I'm only being practical. Let's face it, we've made a lot of

effort lately, but what's the satisfaction ratio? Nil. It's almost a
case for an emergency board meeting.

LAURIE: Oh, very lyrical! Don't you get excited or anything, will
you? Don't you dare get optimistic, you might burst a blood vessel.

BILL: Ideas is one thing, execution's another.

LAURIE: Oh, we've had a run of bad luck, I admit. But this is a
winner. A winner! Imagine it...the sort of women you don't meet
at the Mecca Ballroom. One of them middle-aged, middle-class
women, with little creases round her eyes, and lines on her neck...

(Lights stay on, but the spotlight picks out a WOMAN wearing a
slip, who addresses LAURIE from the blank area.)

WOMAN: You mustn't think I'm a whore, Laurie...I know I hardly
know you...it probably seems strange that I should suddenly ask
you into my bedroom. But I'm not a whore. I'm a married woman
with children and I love my husband. I think he's tired of me,
Laurie. When I saw you I knew you'd understand, I could see you
were going to be the one. Try to love me a little. I know I'm not
young any more, and there are creases in my face. But I'm not
old...you do want me, don't you, Laurie?

SCENE FOUR

The slamming of an offstage front door ends this scene. The spot goes
off.

LAURIE: Fuck, I was enjoying that.

(Enter LAURIE's MUM, a slim, neat woman about 46. She moves
with energetic, precise actions contrasting with LAURIE's heavy
lethargy.)

MUM: How's your dad?

LAURIE: Sinking fast.

MUM: What?

LAURIE: His eyes have misted over. His feet have gone cold.

MUM: Laurie!

LAURIE: Look, I haven't seen him, so how can I tell you?

MUM (removing coat): I think you might have had the decency to take
a look in now and again, I don't ask you to do much...

LAURIE: Why don't you sit down? You've only just got in.

MUM: How can I?

LAURIE (standing up to demonstrate): You bend your legs and you go -

MUM: He's in terrible pain, Laurie.

LAURIE: Well, he's dying, isn't he? What can he expect? If he will die, he has to face the consequences.

MUM: He is your father.

LAURIE: That's nothing to go wild about, is it? I think there ought to be some sort of government grant for people like me, you know, a sort of compensation for people with fathers like him. I might have been nice looking with a different old man. I might have been another Warren Beatty. Oh no, I have to have a gargoyle for a father.

MUM: You should be ashamed of yourself, in front of Bill.

LAURIE: Bill don't mind.

MUM: You've no right to be so bloody superior. You haven't got two halfpennies to rub together. At least your dad wasn't afraid of a day's work.

LAURIE: Let's face it, the quicker he gets borne aloft the better it is for both of us. You for a start because –

MUM: I'm not listening to you!

LAURIE: He's a millstone. A millstone. You could have gone places with the right old man. He's not even in your class, you're intelligent, you got looks, and what's he got? He's a bloody moron, he is.

MUM: You never –

LAURIE: I have, I have tried to look beyond the frayed braces and the carpet slippers, and the trousers round his bloody neck, but there's nothing there. Nothing.

SCENE FIVE

In the dark space DAD appears, dressed as described, with a cigarette in the corner of his mouth. He holds a racing paper.

DAD: I got a tip for Nestor for the 3.30. I like its form, from what I can see, but I ain't no good at form, it's too complicated for me, all them little figures get on my nerves. I'll watch it on the box this afternoon, maybe. I'll kip before the bloody late shift starts. 'Ere, is my bloody dinner ready?

(The light goes out.)

SCENE SIX

Action continues from Scene Four.

MUM: If you're too mean to show a bit of sympathy to someone in pain, I can.

(Exits.)

LAURIE: Join the Pepsi generation! She wasted her time with him, chucked her life away. You know, she could have got a really nice feller for a husband, but she had to pick on him. She's good-looking, isn't she?

BILL: Yeah...

LAURIE: Here, look at this.

(He gets a photograph from the table drawer.)

See. Apart from the clothes, she was all right, wasn't she?

BILL: Kept her figure.

LAURIE: Nice looking, eh?

BILL: Bloody nice.

LAURIE: And then she marries him. It was the war. They were friends, always met at the bus stop or something, and he was crazy about her. When he wasn't kipping, I suppose. And then when the war started, she felt sorry for him, thought he was being sent away or something, so they got hitched. Of course, being the lousy, cheating bastard that he is, he got turned down instead of going off and getting killed like everybody else. And there she was - lumbered.

BILL: She's got a bit of class, your mum.

LAURIE: Came from a wealthy family. All gone now though. I expect her dad went on the drink when he saw what she was marrying.

BILL: Pity. I mean about the money.

LAURIE: We'll make it, don't worry. As soon as he throws off the mortal coils, we'll be in for a bit. It's inevitable, he never spent a penny on us. With that to kick us off, I forsee an idle, sexy future for the pair of us. And of course, a chintzy little pad for my mum.

BILL: A good class of tart...

LAURIE: The very cream of call girls. Dial-a-shag, in my tasteful country home.

BILL: Weekend parties with two or three whores. Maybe a black one.

LAURIE: You've got the picture. And how do we achieve maximum profitability with minimum effort? How do we come into loads of loot without lifting more than a couple of fingers? I'll tell you. The first thing you get clear in your head is that you've got nothing to offer anybody. You are A1 ordinary, you have achieved maximum mediocrity. Right?

BILL: Right.

LAURIE: So there are a couple of ways open to you. One is crime.

BILL: Crime?

LAURIE: But that's not for me. Not that there's any risk, it's just that criminals haven't got any class. Take the Krays. The only other thing is property. Property gives us all the time in the world to get after those sweet little scrubbers.

BILL: It's a lovely idea, but it's not that easy. Who's going to give a mortgage to a layabout like you?

LAURIE: I'm not incapable of working for a month or two. We'll make the repayments out of the rent. You see, the thing to do is to get hold of some bleeding great Victorian house and let it out to students and immigrants. They live anywhere, don't they? Don't bother to tell me it's not allowed under the mortgage, I know that, but who's going to know? You have to use your imagination, if everyone stuck to the rules there wouldn't be half the number of millionaires there are today. Rules are made to be broken.

BILL: And him up there - he's leaving enough for the deposit?

LAURIE: He might have left it to my mum, but I can talk her round. It's so bloody easy it's ridiculous! We need never do a day's work for the rest of our lives. Do you realize that? Have you had a glimpse of our beautiful prospects?

BILL: He might hang on for years.

LAURIE: With what he's got? He's got the dreaded, hasn't he?

BILL: How long?

LAURIE: Couple of days. He's not even conscious half the time... his eyelids are like little pink butterflies, all translucent, hovering on the brink of destruction...

BILL: I see.

LAURIE: That suits you, does it? Meets with your approval?

BILL: Well, the way I see it -

LAURIE: How do you see it?

BILL: Well, if he's in pain, it's good for all concerned. Isn't it?

LAURIE: Oh, yes, you were thinking of him, of course. That's very considerate of you. You don't like to think of him in pain, I can see that.

BILL: I'm all for euthanasia.

LAURIE: Oh, naturally.

BILL: People have a right to it.

LAURIE: Not him. He doesn't deserve to drift out of life in a hazy dream. Fuck him. When I think how he used to treat us, the miserable cunt. Straight in from work, stuffs his gut, hardly a word from one year to the next. He was selfish to the last hair on his balls. Come to think of it, I'm not sure he was really human. He did have hairy legs, but I never noticed his feet. I reckon he had little hooves.

(Enter MUM.)

MUM: He's resting. When I went in, you know, he looked up, and his eyes were full of tears...

LAURIE: Ahhh...

MUM: I'd like you to see him.

LAURIE: Me?

MUM: You heard.

LAURIE: What for?

MUM: To please me.

LAURIE: You really want me to?

MUM: For God's sake –

LAURIE: All right, all right, all right. I'll take a little look. Only from the door, mind you.

(Exit LAURIE. A pause.)

BILL: Happy release for you... I expect... I mean, it'll take a load off your mind if he... won't it?

MUM: I don't know what I'll do.

BILL: Rest yourself, get over it. Change of scene, like...

MUM: I suppose I have got used to the idea he might... might not be with us for long. When it comes I expect I'll be more or less resigned.

BILL: Could be a new lease of life... if you look on the best side of it.

MUM: I do try to.

(She gets up, brushes her hair in the mirror.)

I don't intend to let the grass grow under my feet. There's plenty a woman of my age can do. I don't think of myself as old, you might do, but –

BILL: No, no, I don't think you're old.

MUM: No?

BILL: No, really. Not at all old.

(Pause.)

MUM: When you get to my age... you see things in a different light, that's all. I'm forty-three this July.

BILL: You look young.

MUM: Forty-three. It's not a bad age for a woman.

BILL: Very good age.

MUM: If you've kept yourself smart.

BILL: And you have.

MUM: A woman can keep her looks if she makes an effort.

BILL: Laurie was showing me a photo –

MUM: Oh, that old photograph! He hangs onto that for some reason. I wish he'd throw it away. I look ghastly!

BILL: No, I was only thinking that –

(Enter LAURIE, flinging himself in chair.)

LAURIE: He was very uncommunicative. Most unfriendly. Not a word, not a murmur from his lips. And there I was, hovering at the bed-side, a ministering angel of mercy!

MUM: You didn't wake him up, he was asleep!

LAURIE: He wasn't asleep! He had an eye open. Just this one eye, staring at me... uagh!

MUM: If you upset him –

LAURIE: I was conspicuous for my self-restraint.

MUM (adopting a light tone, for BILL): We had some good years... do you remember Lyme Regis?

LAURIE: 'Course I remember Lyme Regis.

MUM: All that candyfloss he bought you...

LAURIE: He knew it would make me sick. That's why he did it.

MUM: Don't be unfair!

LAURIE: He knew I was intelligent, and he hated that. He couldn't forgive me for that. When he looked at me there were 'O' levels engraved on my forehead.

MUM: Laurie –

LAURIE: He couldn't hold a conversation, could he? He was incapable of putting words together. And when he saw us talking! He was frothing at the gob! He was, he was epileptic!

MUM: Don't tell bloody lies!

BILL (standing up): I'm afraid I've got to be off.

MUM: Oh...

LAURIE: Come again, as the actress said to the bishop.

BILL: Ta ta. 'Bye, Mrs Wyman.

MUM: Goodbye, Bill.

(Exit BILL. A pause.)

LAURIE: We'll have a good time, won't we, eh? When it's all over.
Restaurants, theatres. See a bit of life.

MUM: You're staying on here, are you?

LAURIE: 'Course I am. I've got plans, of course.

MUM: What plans?

LAURIE: Plans.

MUM: What plans?

LAURIE: A few ideas. You'll be all right.

MUM: You could get a job for a start.

LAURIE: Oh, Muriel...

MUM: Get a position in life.

LAURIE: Have I got ulcers? Am I run down? Do I look sad?

MUM: You'll have to sometime!

LAURIE: I don't share that view. No, that's an opinion I don't hold.

MUM: What the hell are you going to do?

LAURIE: Look, your worries are over, all bar the Funeral Games.

MUM: I'm not worrying, I'm interested, that's all.

LAURIE: I've got whole regiments of brain cells sweating over the
problem at this very minute. I can assure you, the future is rosy,
for both of us. Now, no more questions.

(He gets a bottle and two glasses.)

Tell me something. Ever since I was a tiny tot I've wondered how
a nice girl like you got lumbered with the living death up there.
How did it happen? I mean, you were good looking –

MUM: I still am, aren't I?

LAURIE: You are, you are! You're a kind of healthy Marlene Dietrich.

MUM: Some of the officers were nice to me in the war. I was popular in the Operations Room.

LAURIE: Go on...

MUM: Oh, they asked me out to dinner, they wanted to take me on the town... there was one who was really keen on me. He was American ... or Canadian... he was a charmer...

SCENE SEVEN

In the blank space of the stage a spotlight reveals a fat AMERICAN OFFICER, standing with his arms on his hips.

OFFICER: Muriel, you're swell, just swell. You know, when I came into the Operations Room, you know what the first thing I said was? Do you know?

(MURIEL, still sitting in the main set, shakes her head.)

I said, hey, who's that swell chick standing over there? I just got to know who she is. I didn't say, what's the news today? I said, hey, who's that swell chick standing over there? That's what I said.

(LAURIE makes a sign of boredom.)

She brightens the place up, I said. She's a ray of golden sunshine. I could almost forget the war was on, in fact, I did forget the war was on. You're sure some doll. Come on, let's go buy a hamburger, Muriel.

MURIEL: Thank you, Hank, but really, I'm due home at once. Another time maybe –

OFFICER: But Muriel –

MURIEL: Another time.

(The spotlight goes out.)

SCENE EIGHT

LAURIE and MUM are together as at the end of Scene Six.

LAURIE: If you liked him you should have gone. You should have packed your bags and gone.

MUM: I was married...

LAURIE: Take what you can get out of life, Muriel, don't let anything stand in the way. You were a mug. If you've got the nerve you can do anything.

MUM: He was very good to me, your dad. He wasn't sophisticated –

LAURIE: He was thick.

MUM: He was kind in his way... he wasn't smart... he adored me
though, oh, he did adore me!

SCENE NINE

DAD is standing in the spotlight wearing a creased 1940's suit, with a
bunch of drooping flowers in one hand and a box of chocolates with a
bow in the other. He is rather hangdog in expression.

DAD: Oh, Muriel, you've come. I was waiting, like you said. I thought
I had the wrong place, the wrong bus stop. I got the tickets. They're
the best. Don't feel you have to come, if there's something more
important... I can pass them on. You look a picture, Muriel, if
you don't mind me saying. I can't stop thinking how lucky I am. I
am, I'm the luckiest bloke I know. Just a minute, Muriel, I've got
something to say. I wanted to say this. What I mean is, I want
you to know you can... rely on me. I'm here, if you need me.
You know? I'll always be here.

(The light goes out. MURIEL is smiling condescendingly.)

SCENE TEN

Action continues from Scene Eight.

LAURIE: He must have needed artificial respiration when you said
you'd marry him. You were a silly cow.

MUM: How dare you!

LAURIE: Ugh, it's obscene, it is, it's obscene!

MUM: Shut your mouth!

(She slaps him.)

LAURIE: Anyway, how much has he got to leave?

MUM: You needn't think you're going to –

LAURIE: I asked. I enquired. I didn't make any propositions, did I?
Did I make any propositions? I asked, purely for information.

MUM: As long as you don't think –

LAURIE: Now, Muriel, I think you can rely on me to respect my dear
father's wishes when it comes to his worldly goods. I can only act
in an advisory capacity.

MUM: I'm not talking money.

(She gets up.)

Now be a bit useful and lay the table, I'm all behind.

(She looks in the mirror.)

LAURIE: As the actress said to the bishop. You relax, you're under a terrible strain. I'd hate you to have a breakdown. Just relax,

(He pushes her gently into a chair.)

...put your feet up,

(He lifts her feet onto a stool.)

...and leave everything to Laurie.

(Lights go down swiftly.)

Act Two

SCENE ONE

On a predominantly dark stage, LAURIE and BILL are sitting in the front of a car, LAURIE at the wheel. At this point the car is stationary, as revealed by dialogue and actions. When the car is moving, sound might help to establish this. At the opening of the scene, BILL is obviously bored, LAURIE is actively observant.

BILL (after a pause): Let's jack it in, shall we? Get a drink? How about a drink?

LAURIE: Anything to avoid the action. Anything to get out of it.

BILL: I'm just as keen as you are - if it's practical.

LAURIE: You know, you don't deserve to get on in life. You really don't. You're a deviationist. You just haven't got the cheek.

BILL: I don't mind trying anything if -

LAURIE: Over there! All right? What do you think?

BILL: Okay, I suppose...

LAURIE (amazed): Okay?

BILL: We've got the whole evening. Come back later.

LAURIE: And turn down good stuff like that?

BILL: I don't seem interested tonight...

LAURIE: What the fuck did you come out for then? What'd you come out for if you're not interested? I don't see the logic...I'm baffled!

BILL: Okay, okay, if you must –

LAURIE: Yes, I must, I definitely must. I can't say no to stuff like that. I'm drawn by an irresistible force.

(He starts the engine and begins to drive.)

Now, wind your window down and get ready. And don't take no for an answer. There's no such word as far as you're concerned. When they say no they mean yes.

(LAURIE looks in the mirror, waving a vehicle behind on frantically.)

Fuck, there's a bus on my tail! Get off, you cunt! Oh, go on, pass me you great turd! Oh, it's sunk in ..

(LAURIE is slowing down, pulling into the kerb at a snail's pace.)

Now, here's your chance –

(Two girls, JANICE and ADELE, are walking slowly along the pavement, pretending to be oblivious of the car crawling along the kerb. They are dressed in garish clothes, eg, yellow, purple coats and shoes. BILL, in the passenger seat of the car, is nearest to them. They are in a separate spotlight, which can be switched off to obliterate them. It is important they should be walking along, eg, on the spot.)

Well say something! Oh, for Christ's sake, speak! Let 'em hear you!

BILL: They're not that great...

LAURIE: Say something!

BILL: I'm not keen!...

LAURIE: Oh fuck, oh Jesus!

(The car revs up.

Switch off spot on girls, indicating they have been left behind.)

Did we look stupid! We looked – we were complete, fetid, steaming turds! What's the matter with you for Christ's sake? They were the best birds we've ever seen on this road! Are you aware of that? Has that penetrated to your microscopic brain?

BILL: I'm sorry, I chickened out, I –

LAURIE: Have we got so many women we can afford to chicken out if the feeling takes you? Have we? Have we got any women at all? I haven't seen women like that since –

BILL: We'll go back!

LAURIE: Go back? Are you kidding? That'll look great, won't it, that'll really impress 'em!

BILL: If they're so great –

LAURIE: You just sat there, your head lolling on your shoulders...
you were spastic, tubular steel spastic!

BILL: I said, we'll go back!

LAURIE: All right.

(Pause.)

BILL: So we're going back?

LAURIE: If you don't feel up to it –

(He reverses the car.)

if the young ladies in their frilly skin tight pants make you feel un-
comfortable –

(They drive on.)

I'll do the talking. I'll talk and drive. You just keep your window
down.

BILL: I'll look stupid. I'll do the talking.

LAURIE: Sure you can manage it? I wouldn't be surprised someone
with a bit of gumption has snapped 'em up by now. Oh, no, there
they are, strolling along, they're fucking begging for it!

(They look sideways as they pass. LAURIE turns the car round
again. These manoeuvres don't involve turning the prop, merely
suitable actions by the actors, such as looking over their shoulders.)

Right now. Play it by ear. Remember, don't take no for an answer.
Keep on.

(Lights on JANICE and ADELE, strolling as before. BILL speaks
through the window of the car.)

BILL: Want a lift? Do you want a lift? Come on.

(To LAURIE.)

Come on, let's leave it –

LAURIE (leaning across, with occasional glance at the road): Here,
darlings! Come and meet two lovely fellas. Don't worry, you're
good enough. Buy you a drink. How's that for bribery? You might
not get another chance.

(Pause.)

Now listen, I'm very tenacious. I've been called the Bulldog by my
friends. I have. What's your name? Haven't you got names?

BILL: Give up, eh –

LAURIE: You must have a name, here, canary, what do they call you,
then?

BILL: Leave it, Laurie –

LAURIE: If you don't get in this lovely car I might lose my temper. I might. And as I'm such a nice person that would be a shame, wouldn't it? Hey, take my tip and get in. That's free advice.

(Pause.)

You know, I think I'm going to have to come and get you... I'm keeping on at you till you get in.

JANICE: There's traffic lights up there, clever Dick.

LAURIE: I shall have to go through 'em, won't I? As it's an emergency.

(The girls laugh.)

Could be a nasty accident. You wouldn't like that on your conscience, would you?

JANICE (to ADELE): Shall we?

LAURIE: Of course you will.

ADELE: All right, but where we going?

LAURIE: We're only local boys.

JANICE: Buy us a drink?

LAURIE: Name the place.

ADELE: They've got to take us to the Swan.

(The girls climb in the back.)

LAURIE: We'll overlook your bad taste.

JANICE: Charming! Here, you stopped before, didn't you?

LAURIE: We did stop, but then we went on again.

ADELE (sourly): Goods weren't up to standard?

LAURIE: More or less, but we forgot we had to buy his granny a Guinness. She's lost without her Guinness. Her head's full of Guinness.

JANICE: You were quick!

LAURIE: His granny's got a big gob!

(Squeals of laughter.)

What are your names, girls?

JANICE: Janice.

LAURIE: Charming...

JANICE: She's Adele...

LAURIE: I'm Laurie. This is Bill.

JANICE: Pleased to meet you.

ADELE: Here, where are we going?

LAURIE: We won't bother with the Swan. It's time you drank in a place with a bit of class.

ADELE: Swan suits us, thanks. You said you were going to the Swan.

LAURIE: I did say that, but I'm very unreliable. Never trust men.

ADELE: We happen to be meeting someone at the Swan.

JANICE: They can wait, Del...

LAURIE: Always another time, Del...

JANICE: Here! You ain't half driving fast!

LAURIE: I'm reckless, too.

JANICE: Don't drink and drive!

LAURIE: That's what they say! Here, two wheels in a minute! Two wheels!

(Shrieks from JANICE.)

I can drive this with my eyes shut.

JANICE: Go on, then.

LAURIE: Think you can take it?

JANICE: Try me!

LAURIE: I will, don't worry!

JANICE: Cheeky!

LAURIE: There you are, eyes shut! All right? Eyes shut.

ADELE: Where are we going?

LAURIE: Don't know, I got my eyes shut!

JANICE: Liar!

ADELE: I want to know where we're going.

JANICE: Oh, Del...

ADELE: I've got a right to know.

LAURIE: Not scared of boys, are you, Del?

ADELE: Certainly not.

LAURIE: Bill'll look after you, won't you, Bill? You'll look after Del?

ADELE: Spare yourself the trouble.

LAURIE: He won't mind.

ADELE: No thanks.

(Engine sounds to establish a rough gradient.)

Here, where are we?

LAURIE: Nearly there.

ADELE: Where the hell are we?

JANICE: Where's the pub?

LAURIE (switches off engine): Five minutes walk.

ADELE: No thanks.

JANICE: Del!

LAURIE: A little walk never hurt anybody. People rely on public transport too much these days. In a few generations human beings won't have any legs.

ADELE: I'll stay here.

JANICE: Oh, come on, Del.

ADELE: I don't want to go, you go.

JANICE: Don't be silly, Del...

LAURIE: Don't you want to stretch your legs?

ADELE: Nope.

LAURIE: She doesn't want to.

(Pause.)

BILL: You go, we'll stay here.

ADELE: No thanks, you go.

JANICE: Del, don't be stupid. She gets like this sometimes.

LAURIE: Come on.

(He gets out. JANICE follows suit. BILL is uncertain what to do, and gets no advice from LAURIE. So he just sits there.

LAURIE and JANICE walk slowly offstage, whence come sounds of giggling. ADELE lights a cigarette. A pause, then a growing atmosphere of panic.)

JANICE: Hey!

LAURIE: What's the matter?

JANICE: Pack that in!

LAURIE: Pack what in?

JANICE: Oh, stop... for Christ's sake! Oh!

(BILL gets out of the car.)

BILL: Laurie? Laurie? Where are you?

JANICE: Del! Del! Oh, God!

BILL: Laurie?

(ADELE leaps out of the car.)

ADELE: I'll get the police, Jan! I'll get the police!

BILL: Hey! It's all right! Here –

(ADELE runs offstage.)

Laurie, for Christ's sake! Laurie!

JANICE: Help!

(BILL moves off in the direction of the sound and is almost knocked over by a fleeing and undressed JANICE who stops to shout back.)

We'll get the police! We'll get you, you fucking bastard! You dirty fucking bastard!

(LAURIE appears. JANICE rushes off. BILL stops him following her.)

BILL: Let's get going, come on, let's go!

LAURIE: Did you see her? Were you looking? Fuck her!

(He bangs on the car roof.)

Did you fucking see it?

BILL: Laurie –

LAURIE: Did you see her legs? Fuck her!

(He leans on the roof.)

I couldn't keep my fucking hands off her. Did you have a good look at her? Oh, God!

BILL: Let's go, Laurie...

LAURIE: I was right there, I could have done it, I was there! Oh, Christ, Jesus Christ...

SCENE TWO

The living room set. A pause before sound of a front door slamming.

DAD (off): Muriel?

(Enter MUM. She removes her coat and headscarf.)

Muriel?

(And brushes her hair.)

Muriel?

(Turning her head from side to side to examine her profile.)

Muriel!

(She puts the brush down.)

Muriel!

(And pulling down her skirt, goes off. There is a pause after the sound of her footsteps have passed overhead. Then her footsteps on the stair are heard again, but slowly. There is an occasional bumping sound and a groan before she enters, assisting an emaciated DAD, wearing slippers and dressing gown. She helps him into a chair.)

MUM: This chair?

(They move on round the room.)

This one? Don't you want this one? Which one do you want?

(He opts for the first.)

Your own chair, you want your own chair.

DAD: Why not? What's wrong with my chair?

MUM: I was thinking this one was nearer.

DAD: Give us your arm. No...no...put your arm round...

(He falls into the chair.)

MUM: Are you warm enough?

(His head falls to one side.)

I don't think I should have brought you down. I really don't. He did say not to move, didn't he? He said you're better off in bed. Here, I'll put a coat –

DAD: No!

MUM: You want to keep warm, don't you? Oh, all right.

(She takes the coat out.)

You're so stubborn, you won't take advice. You will make yourself worse. Now look, you're sinking down the chair.

(She goes to help, but he brushes her away.)

Oh, all right, slide down if you like! There, you have slid down, you're nearly on the floor. Shall I put you up? Well, do you want me to help you? Do you?

(Pause.)

Look, I only want to help!

DAD: The pain, Muriel...

MUM: Oh, I know...

(She stands helplessly looking at him.)

Let someone help you then.

DAD: You can't help.

(She sits down with a magazine.)

MUM: I don't know why you wanted to come down, I don't. You can't do any good down here, you can't possibly be comfortable.

(Pause.)

Quite honestly, I think it's selfish. Supposing Laurie comes in with some friends? It wouldn't look very nice, would it? What would they think, with you stuck there? It'd be quite a shock. I do think you might have thought of that.

(A long pause. She reads. He droops.)

DAD: You're provided for. You do know that, don't you?

MUM: Thank you, Vic.

DAD: I wouldn't leave you with nothing.

MUM: Of course not, Vic.

DAD: Whatever happened, I wouldn't leave my wife with nothing.

MUM: No...

DAD: No, I wouldn't.

(Pause.)

Someone'll come along, I expect. As soon as I'm out the way. As soon as yer back's turned.

MUM: Vic!

DAD: We all know, don't we? We know how it is.

MUM: Do be quiet!

DAD: Yer wife's never yer own.

MUM: Will you shut up!

DAD: How long will it be, eh? How long before he's up there in my place, doing things to you!

MUM: You talk a lot of bloody nonsense! Do you hear?

(Pause.)

DAD: I know, I've seen it. During the war. I'm not silly, Muriel. I've seen it on the job too, as soon as they're out the way...

SCENE THREE

In the blank part of the stage a spotlight reveals the U.S. OFFICER from Scene Seven of the previous act.

He steps forward.

MURIEL: Shh!

OFFICER: Why?

MURIEL: He's sleeping.

OFFICER: He looks like he couldn't raise a finger, let alone –

MURIEL: Hank, I –

OFFICER (about to embrace her): Honey, I can show you a good time. We can make it together. You gotta drop this schmultz, you gotta come all the way with me. Muriel, I could just die looking at your ass the way you cross that Operations Room, you know I could bust my trouser buttons!

MURIEL: Hank, you make me feel like a woman!

OFFICER: I want you and you want me and nothing's gonna stand in our way!

(He hugs her.)

MURIEL: Oh, Hank, you've got a way with you, you've got everything a woman needs!

(He puts his hand up her skirt but the lights go down. When they come up again MURIEL is in her chair.)

SCENE FOUR

MUM: You're sliding down again.

DAD: I don't care... I don't care about nothing.

MUM: That's right, you get well.

(Pause.)

I was thinking of tinting my hair. Would you like that? Just a streak of ash blonde. I've always wanted a streak. Be nice, wouldn't it? I've often fancied a streak. But you want to sleep, don't you?

(She gets up.)

Shall I pull the curtains? You don't want the light in your eyes. There, how's that?

(The room is nearly dark.

Enter LAURIE with a slam.)

LAURIE: Christ, I'm in a coalmine! Here, what's the curtains pulled for? Lights!

(He goes to the window, draws back curtains.)

MUM: Your Dad's sleeping!

LAURIE: What the hell is he doing down here? Can't have him dying in the front room, it's infra dig.

MUM: He was feeling a bit cut off...

LAURIE: I'm not eating my dinner with him lying here like that... puts me off my food.

MUM: Leave him alone, Laurie –

LAURIE (bending to pick up his father): He's going back where he came from.

MUM: For God's sake!

LAURIE (lifting him by numbers): Hup, one, two, over, one, two. Out, one two...

(He goes off with DAD, calling step. Footsteps overhead, fading, then returning.)

LAURIE: He's losing weight, that's one relief.

MUM (putting coat on): Your dinner's in the oven. I'll be late for work if I hang about.

(LAURIE exits right. Returns with a plate and knife and fork. He starts eating at the table. His mother ties a headscarf and picks up a bag.)

I'm off, then.

LAURIE: Right.

MUM: Ta ta.

(Exit MUM.

LAURIE eats at a very leisurely pace, picking at the food, stabbing at it with his fork, gazing idly out of the window. Suddenly he sees something which rivets his attention. He watches for a moment and then exits quickly. There is a pause, a distant conversation, then SHIRLEY enters, followed by LAURIE. She is about 25, with permed hair and a round, attractive face. She is dressed very plainly, perhaps in trousers.)

SHIRLEY: Are you sure it's all right?

LAURIE: 'Course I am. We've been neighbours for years, haven't we?

SHIRLEY: Suppose we have.

LAURIE: Take a seat.

SHIRLEY (perching): Thanks...

LAURIE: Quite a handful, with the baby, is it?

SHIRLEY: Oh, yes...

(A pause, while LAURIE looks at SHIRLEY appreciatively.)

SHIRLEY: I –

LAURIE: We – after you.

SHIRLEY: Oh, I was just going to say... I heard your dad was ill.

LAURIE: Not ill, dying.

SHIRLEY: Oh dear... that's dreadful...

LAURIE: It is a shame. Would you like a drink?

SHIRLEY: Thank you.

(LAURIE draws a couple of bottles out from under the chair.)

LAURIE: Gin and tonic? Rum and coke? Got Baccardi if you fancy it.

SHIRLEY: Oh, thanks.

(He opens the bottles, dusts a couple of tumblers with a handkerchief.)

LAURIE: Funny, isn't it? All these years and we never said a word.

SHIRLEY: It is strange.

LAURIE: Weird.

SHIRLEY: Mmm...

LAURIE: I mean, if baby's ball hadn't bounced over the fence we might never have got round to it.

SHIRLEY: Funny.

LAURIE: Not that I haven't noticed you, hanging out washing, playing with baby and that.

SHIRLEY: Oh?

LAURIE: Oh yes, I noticed. I'm at home a lot, see.

SHIRLEY: That's nice.

LAURIE: I haven't got a job... in the ordinary sense.

SHIRLEY: That's nice.

LAURIE: It is nice.

(Pause.)

SHIRLEY: What are you in then?

LAURIE: Property.

SHIRLEY: Property?

LAURIE (sitting down): Got a few places here and there...

SHIRLEY: Lucky thing...

LAURIE: I am lucky. I never fancied slogging my guts out at some bench. That's all right if you've got no ambition. It's all right for them with no drive.

SHIRLEY: Oh...

LAURIE: I'm not greedy for money... it just keeps coming in, you know. There's a lot more to life than money.

SHIRLEY: Oh, yes.

LAURIE: Reading, for example...

SHIRLEY: Yes...

LAURIE: The thing about being in property is it gives you time to read.

SHIRLEY: Oh yes...

LAURIE: I'm glad you agreed. How about another drink?

SHIRLEY: Can't leave baby on her own...

LAURIE: Home all the time, are you?

SHIRLEY: Well, baby –

LAURIE: Must get a drag...

SHIRLEY: She's a handful.

LAURIE: I bet... I've often thought I'd come out and say hello. Go on, I say to myself, go and say hello.

SHIRLEY: Oh?

LAURIE: You can live right next door to someone and never get acquainted. That's the trouble with society. People are too isolated. They're scared of each other.

SHIRLEY: Mmm...

LAURIE: Scared of getting involved.

SHIRLEY: Yeah...

LAURIE: What do you think?

SHIRLEY: Could be.

LAURIE: Yeah, but what do you think? Why don't they get involved? Do you feel like getting involved?

SHIRLEY: Me?

LAURIE: Why do you want to get involved?

SHIRLEY: I didn't say anything about –

LAURIE: We're both looking for involvement, let's face it, I've been looking at you for a couple of years and saying to myself I wouldn't half like getting my hands round her –

SHIRLEY: I think I'll be going, thank you –

(She gets up.)

LAURIE: Every time you bent over to pick up a bit of washing I was getting all tight in the chest, here. Why do you think I rushed out to get that ball this afternoon? Not so baby could carry on with her game, don't worry, it was so I could start mine!

SHIRLEY: I think you're stark –

LAURIE (facing her): You're dying to get involved with me!

SHIRLEY: You're crazy! You're a nut!

LAURIE: What sort of life have you got, eh? I'm not surprised you want to get involved. Nights round the tele, mowing the lawn on Sunday, that's not a life, is it? That's not living.

SHIRLEY: Suits us.

LAURIE: Purgatory, that is.

SHIRLEY: I didn't come to be insulted.

LAURIE: No, you came to be seduced, didn't you? That's why you came.

SHIRLEY: By you? Don't make me laugh!

LAURIE: You're sex-starved!

SHIRLEY: I am?

LAURIE: How often do you get it, eh? Once a month?

SHIRLEY: You keep your dirty, horrible ideas to yourself! I wouldn't give you a second look. Who do you think you are?

LAURIE: Your golden opportunity. Tonight's Star Prize.

SHIRLEY: Pathetic!

LAURIE: Your loss, darling!

SHIRLEY: Get lost!

LAURIE: Chance of a lifetime...

SHIRLEY: You really think you're clever, don't you? You really think you're something –

LAURIE: I'm realistic.

SHIRLEY (going out): Take a look at yourself some time!

LAURIE (shouting): You're not Brigitte Bardot yourself, you old hag!

SHIRLEY (off): Have to be an old hag to want you!

LAURIE (an afterthought): Love to Dada!

(Left alone, LAURIE pours himself a drink and collapses into a chair. Lights fade for late afternoon. Sudden doorbell arouses him. He exits, returns with BILL.)

BILL: How's he doing?

LAURIE (in chair again): Clinging.

BILL: Who's been drinking?

LAURIE: Me and a woman.

BILL: A woman?

LAURIE: Surprised? I can have a woman in here if I want, can't I?

BILL: You had her?

LAURIE: You don't object, I hope? You don't mind me having a normal healthy sex-life?

BILL: I only asked who –

LAURIE: The lady opposite.

BILL: Christ!

LAURIE: A good general knows when to take his opportunities.

BILL: You actually –

LAURIE: She's not quite so good close up. I admit. One of her eyes is a bit higher than the other, but I wouldn't say it put me off.

BILL: Lucky bastard!

LAURIE: It wasn't luck! It was nerve. I decided to go all out for it, I was that little bit cheeky, and I...I did what comes naturally.

BILL: Tell us about it. Wait a minute, let me get comfortable.

(He sits down.)

LAURIE: I have told you.

BILL: No, the details.

LAURIE: Sod you!

BILL: Oh, come on, I'm jealous, I don't mind telling you.

LAURIE: Don't you worry, with our imagination we'll see the inside of quite a few classy bedrooms before long.

BILL: Saggy bums of middle-aged bags...

LAURIE: Fucking hell! What's wrong with that? You always wanted a middle-aged bag! That's what you said you always wanted!

BILL: Don't get excited! You've had your fun.

LAURIE (calmly): Doesn't mean I can't speculate, does it?

BILL: Bloody greedy you are. Never satisfied.

LAURIE: I want a life of unearned luxury.

BILL: Not getting far with that, are we? We're in a dream world, you and me, drifting along, while fellas younger than us are in the money.

LAURIE: They make the money, we make their wives.

BILL: You might.

LAURIE: You get on my bloody wick the way you go on! They're the failures, not us! They're the berks! They sit in their bloody offices, they stand at their fucking benches, working their lives away. That's not living, is it? Is that what you want? That's life to them, the poor sods, they don't know any different, but you and me, we've got the precious gift of insight, haven't we? We've got ideas, haven't we? We've got the cheek to go out there and make it out of berks like them, so we never have to lift a sodding finger, so we can screw till the bloody cows come home!

BILL: All right, all right.

LAURIE: I tell you, we're okay, we're on our way as soon as he kicks it. You ought to be bloody grateful I'm cutting you in on this. Fucked if I know why.

BILL: I'm not ungrateful. I get depressed.

LAURIE: Get depressed somewhere else.

BILL: It's the dole that depresses me.

LAURIE: You'll be having treatment the way you carry on. Manic depression. They put little wires in your head and shove hundreds of volts through you. You just catch a whiff of burning brain cells ... what you need is a bit of success, the sort of success that makes a mess of clean white sheets.

BILL: An afternoon in bed.

LAURIE: Behind every great man there lies a scrubber. And behind every scrubber is a behind.

(Door slams. Enter MUM.)

MUM: Hello, Bill.

BILL: Hello, Mrs Wyman.

MUM: Muriel's the name.

BILL: Oh...

MUM: I expect you two are waiting round for your tea.

LAURIE: A woman's work is never done.

MUM: The wind's terrible today.

(That mirror again.)

Look at me, my eyes are all smarting...I look a mess. Is your mum a mess, Bill?

BILL: Yeah...

MUM: Still, we do our best, don't we? Patch up the old crate.

(She brushes her hair.)

Try not to look hideous. Now I'll have to go up to him.

LAURIE: Don't overdo the Florence Nightingale!

(MUM has gone out.)

You know what I feel like now? Real degradation, you know, sweat and crudity...

BILL: After this afternoon?

LAURIE: I'm funny like that.

(Pause.)

What's keeping her? Maybe he's dead. Lying there, half out the bed, with one arm dangling...

(Pause.)

Too arty for him. More likely crapped himself.

BILL: Dirty bugger!

LAURIE: He's got no right to hang on like this, when we're waiting for his money...

BILL: Wants his three score and ten, doesn't he?

LAURIE: No, it's half price at the cinema he's worried about.

(Pause.)

They were a thick lot that generation, a really pin-headed outfit ...mind you, he was outstanding in his way. He got the Most Retarded Employee Award for ten years running at London Transport. That was before the immigrants, of course. Even then he was runner-up. Where is she?

BILL: Ducky, I am star-ving!

LAURIE: She shouldn't be cleaning up after him, it's not her job. He should be on the Health, in some home for incurables. Get his moneysworth then, wouldn't he? He could crap to his heart's content - here a crap, there a crap, nearly everywhere a crap. Here, pass me that broom. We can't have this.

(LAURIE stands on his chair and rams the ceiling with the broom.)

Wakey wakey! Anyone at home?

(He rams again.)

The nerve of him!

(He rams to the tune of:)

Why – are – we – wait – ing, why – are – we waiting?

(Lights off.)

SCENE FIVE

A couple of days might have elapsed. LAURIE is doing press-ups. The doorbell. He finishes his daily twenty before going out to answer.

SHIRLEY (off): Is your mum in?

LAURIE (amazed, and a bit inarticulate): She's...no...

SHIRLEY: No one in?

LAURIE: Only me.

(Pause.)

SHIRLEY: Can I come in?

(Door closes, enter an attractively dressed SHIRLEY, followed by LAURIE.)

Can I sit down?

LAURIE: Yes...of course.

SHIRLEY: I suppose you're surprised to see me.

(He nods.)

You didn't expect me.

(He shakes his head.)

I was thinking...I meant to write or something, and then I was passing by, I thought...well, I'd say it personally.

(LAURIE's gaze travels inevitably to her provocative clothes. A see-through blouse might be appropriate.)

LAURIE: Say what?

SHIRLEY: I'm sorry. For the other day.

LAURIE (ready to take advantage): Oh?

SHIRLEY: Well, I was rude, wasn't I? I'm sorry about that.

LAURIE: Yeah, well...that's all right.

SHIRLEY: I don't know what came over me.

LAURIE: These things happen, don't they?

SHIRLEY: I wasn't my normal self.

LAURIE: Think nothing of it. It's all in the past.

SHIRLEY: I just wanted to make sure we'd still be friends.

LAURIE: Why not?

(Pause.)

SHIRLEY: I'm so glad...

(Pause.)

Well...

LAURIE (rising to his feet): Well, have a drink, will you? What is it?

SHIRLEY: You choose.

LAURIE: Rum and coke?

SHIRLEY: Right first time!

LAURIE: I remembered.

SHIRLEY: You are glad I came back? You knew I would?

LAURIE: I had an inkling.

SHIRLEY: You knew!

LAURIE: Well...not that I was losing any sleep –

SHIRLEY: I bet!

(He hands her a drink.)

LAURIE: Cheers.

SHIRLEY: Here's to us!

(Pause.)

I hope I'm not interrupting anything, I mean, with the property?

LAURIE: Oh no, no...that takes care of itself, mostly. I just...er, I just collect the rent.

SHIRLEY: Lovely.

LAURIE: Not bad.

(Pause.)

SHIRLEY: Must take a bit of doing, property. Got a lot, have you?

LAURIE: Quite a bit.

SHIRLEY: Why do you live in a pokey little house like this?

LAURIE: That's my mum, she likes it here, she won't move. People get attached to houses, don't they?

SHIRLEY: Not attached to mine. They're damp.

LAURIE: Yeah.

SHIRLEY: You get vacant ones, now and again, I suppose?

LAURIE: We have a waiting list, my partner and me.

SHIRLEY: Oh?

LAURIE: Well, they're nice places... Georgian.

SHIRLEY: Smashing.

(LAURIE nods. They drink.)

Not married, then?

LAURIE: Not likely!

SHIRLEY: You don't like it, then?

LAURIE: All right if you're the sort.

SHIRLEY: I don't believe in the restrictions. I think you should be free, you know.

LAURIE: Definitely.

SHIRLEY: One man, one woman, it's a bit, you know...

LAURIE: Stupid.

SHIRLEY: If two people like each other, I don't see why... do you?

LAURIE: Nope.

(Pause.)

SHIRLEY: Don't you want me any more?

LAURIE: I want you all right.

SHIRLEY: I'm not hurrying you? I don't want you to think I'm cheap.

LAURIE: No...

(He puts his glass down, just in time because SHIRLEY flings herself at him.)

SHIRLEY: Upstairs, darling!

LAURIE: He's up there!

SHIRLEY (at his buttons): I don't mind, darling, I don't mind where, oh, Larry!

LAURIE: Laurie!

SHIRLEY: Laurie, you made me feel so wanted! I felt wanted! You made me feel a woman! Undress me, take my clothes off...oh, be gentle with me, my love, my love...

LAURIE: There is one thing – I haven't had a lot of experience...I have had a bit...but...

SHIRLEY: Larry –

LAURIE: Laurie –

SHIRLEY: Take me, Larry!

(They are on the floor, fumbling with their clothes.)

LAURIE: I always fancied you! Always!

SHIRLEY: I love you, I love you...

LAURIE: You're so beautiful, you're lovely, I can't believe how beautiful you are...

SHIRLEY: Say you need me! Say you love my body!

LAURIE: I love you, and your body, and you, always, forever...

SHIRLEY: Darling...

(Discreet fade.)

Act Three

SCENE ONE

MUM is putting the finishing touches to her dress. She is trying on a navy blue straw hat, pinning a brooch to her lapel, adjusting her tights and so on. LAURIE is offstage, in the kitchen shaving. When he appears he is wearing a vest.

LAURIE (off): What are you tarting up for?

MUM: I can look nice, can't I?

LAURIE (off): I said what are you tarted up for?

MUM: Founders Day, or whatever you call it. What do you call it?

LAURIE (off): How do I know? The bathroom's in a mess. What are all these bottles?

MUM: I'll see to it when I come home.

(LAURIE enters, MUM doesn't notice. She carries on obliviously.)

LAURIE: I could fancy you myself.

MUM: Oh! I look nice, do I?

LAURIE (clear case of understatement): All right, yeah...

MUM: Do you think it's discreet enough?

LAURIE: I like hats.

MUM: Is my skirt short enough? I don't want them to think I'm an old fogey.

LAURIE: Just right.

MUM (holding herself stiff): Look at my tiny little waist. I haven't put on an inch since I was married, except when I had you.

(Pause.)

And I'm not wearing a girdle. How many women of my age could say that?

LAURIE: I don't know...

MUM: Do you like my tights?

LAURIE: Yeah...

MUM: Not bad for forty-three?

LAURIE: You're all right...

MUM: Only all right?

LAURIE (going back to kitchen): What do you want me to say?

MUM: Something nice...be a change.

LAURIE (off): All right...you're...you're looking nice...

MUM: I could get away with not wearing a bra. There's nothing saggy about me.

(She lifts her breasts.)

Sir Geoffrey gives a party today. I don't expect much will happen.

(Pause.)

Just a few drinks.

(Pause.)

They're very good employers.

(Pause. A final tweak at her hair.)

Well, I've got to be going. Keep an eye on your dad, there's a good boy. See to his dinner.

LAURIE (off): I'll see to him.

(She exits. LAURIE appears, stands around, then exits again. He reappears buttoning his shirt. The doorbell rings. LAURIE goes out and reappears with SHIRLEY.)

SHIRLEY: I saw your mum go out.

LAURIE (kissing her): You're nice and early.

SHIRLEY (dispassionately): Do you want to start now?

(A pause. LAURIE looks a little surprised.)

LAURIE: Don't you... wouldn't you like a drink?

SHIRLEY (shrugging, sitting down): All right, if you like.

LAURIE (taking bottle out from under chair): How's baby? Haven't left any saucepans on the boil, I hope.

SHIRLEY: She's all right.

(Pause.)

LAURIE: How are you?

SHIRLEY: All right.

(Pause. He gives her a glass, sits on arm of her chair.)

LAURIE: Give us a kiss.

(They kiss.)

Come on.

(They kiss again.)

Yeah, well...

SHIRLEY: I'm not feeling so good today.

LAURIE: I had that impression myself.

SHIRLEY: I'm sorry.

LAURIE (jokily, without bitterness): Can't be helped, once in a while. It's those little hormones, isn't it? Am I right? Some tiny little hormone whizzing round in your womb.

SHIRLEY: Don't be horrible. I've been all right all the week, haven't I? Got no complaints, have you?

LAURIE: No, no, I could definitely recommend you.

SHIRLEY: If you must know, I'm feeling guilty.

LAURIE: Whaat?

SHIRLEY: Guilty!

LAURIE: Just a hormone... it'll go.

SHIRLEY: I've been thinking, and I... feel bad about it.

(Pause.)

LAURIE (seriously): Look here, do you love me, or don't you?

SHIRLEY: 'Course.

LAURIE: And do I love you?

SHIRLEY: S'pose so.

LAURIE (gets up, gesticulates): Well, that's it, then, isn't it? That's all there is to it. I love you and you love me. So we're going to set up together, right?

(Pause.)

SHIRLEY: And what about him?

LAURIE: Well I'm not saying goodbye to you just because of him! He's a loser, as it happens. Tough luck, of course, but we've got ourselves to think of.

SHIRLEY: It's easy for you.

LAURIE: Easy for anyone. I can't see any problem. We're in love, we're happy together. So we go off together. Stands to reason. Take the baby, I said I don't mind the baby.

SHIRLEY: It's not that easy!

LAURIE: It is! It is! If you keep saying that you never get anywhere. You only think it's hard because most people haven't got the guts to go and do what they want!

SHIRLEY: He's been good to me...

LAURIE: I expect he has, but now –

SHIRLEY: We could stay lovers...

LAURIE: You're joking!

SHIRLEY: Could be more exciting that way.

LAURIE: I happen to want you at nights.

SHIRLEY: I could say I'm staying with my mum now and again...

LAURIE: Fucking hell! Don't you understand! What's the matter with you? Stay with your bloody mum!

SHIRLEY: Leave persons out of it!

LAURIE: Look here, it's a fact you only get so many chances in life, you have to grab your chances 'cos if you don't you're a loser. I know that, from experience. You never want to stick with what you've got if something better comes along. No one's going to stop you, it's a free country. It's every man for himself, see? If you don't make it out of someone, he'll make it out of you. Same in personal life, you have to get happiness where you can. Am I right?

SHIRLEY: I still think –

LAURIE: For Christ's sake! You said you loved me!

(Pause.)

SHIRLEY (quietly): You take everything so seriously!

(Pause.)

LAURIE (bruised): Did you say you loved me?

SHIRLEY: I did but –

LAURIE: Did you or didn't you?

SHIRLEY: Yes, but –

LAURIE: No bloody buts!

SHIRLEY: I was excited.

LAURIE: For fuck's sake, either you love me or you don't!

(Pause.)

SHIRLEY: I do, you know I do...

LAURIE: 'Cos I love you... you make me feel good, you make me...
you turn me on, all right? Come on, let's have it...

SHIRLEY: I was wondering –

LAURIE (at her blouse): Come on...

SHIRLEY: I just wondered...

LAURIE: Christ, I could eat you, you're so –

SHIRLEY: I wanted to know if –

LAURIE (hands under skirt): Take 'em off, take 'em off, oh you –

SHIRLEY: Laurie –

(Heavy knocks on the ceiling stop them.)

Whatssat?

LAURIE (at it again): Him, him, it's only him...

SHIRLEY (is now on her back gazing at the source of the noise, not
playing an active part): What's he doing?

LAURIE: Knocking. Come on, here, come on...

(Knocks again.)

SHIRLEY: Hadn't you better –

LAURIE: Fuck him!

SHIRLEY: He might be –

LAURIE: Fuck him!

(Knocks again.)

SHIRLEY: Laurie...

LAURIE (put out at last): Shut up! Shut your bloody row!

SHIRLEY: Laurie!

(And again.)

LAURIE (on his feet): I'll kill him! I'll murder him! He messed my
mum up and now he wants to mess me up too! Shut - your - bleeding
- row!

(A long silence.)

LAURIE (throwing himself in a chair): He's put me off...

SHIRLEY (getting up, rolling up her tights): About them houses...

LAURIE: What houses?

SHIRLEY: All your property.

LAURIE (getting a drink): Oh, that...

SHIRLEY: I was thinking...

(This is difficult for her.)

I was thinking... how about putting me in one of 'em. With him, of
course, and baby. You know how small it is in these places, and
baby needs, well, she needs...

LAURIE (smiling): Come here... give us a kiss...

SHIRLEY (kissed): You will?

LAURIE: Give us a big kiss.

SHIRLEY (kissed): I knew you would, Laurie, you're a good bloke...
you could visit me, it'd be easier -

LAURIE: It's a lovely idea. It's beautiful. Yeah, it is... but I can't
'cos I haven't got one.

SHIRLEY: Couldn't you turn someone out?

LAURIE: I couldn't do that either.

SHIRLEY: You could say they were bad tenants.

LAURIE: No I couldn't.

SHIRLEY: You could!

LAURIE: No...

SHIRLEY: If you love me -

LAURIE: Look, allow me to put you out of your misery. You don't
really think I've got any houses, do you? You didn't really take all
that seriously? You don't think I'd stick in this miserable little
hole, with him up there choking his heart out if I had a bloody
garden shed of my own, let alone a house? Do you? Not so fucking
likely!

(Pause.)

SHIRLEY: You were having me on?

LAURIE: Having you on what?

SHIRLEY: You were leading me on –

LAURIE: A joke, you know?

SHIRLEY (crushed): Why? I don't see it? Why?

LAURIE: I dunno why, I just said it, that's all. Just conversation.
What's it matter? As a matter of fact –

SHIRLEY: What's it matter? What's it matter? Oh, for Christ's sake!

LAURIE: All right, all right.

SHIRLEY (strikes him): You dirty, lying bastard! You sodding liar!
How could you, how could you do it? How could you use me like
that? You stinking bloody pig!

LAURIE: Watch your fucking language, darling!

SHIRLEY (hysteria): To think I let you touch me! I let you see
me! Oh, look at me! I'm half undressed! Oh, my God, my God!
And I've never been unfaithful, never!

LAURIE (trying to figure this out): Tell me, here, what is it? Just
because I'm not rich? Is that it? 'Cos I've got plans –

SHIRLEY: You don't think I'd have gone anywhere with you, do you?
Not if you were the last man on earth! Spend my life with a layabout
like you when I've got the most loving husband in the world and a
darling little girl? I hate your bloody guts, I hate you! Don't come
near me! You've...you've contaminated me!

LAURIE (advancing a pace): You came back to me!

SHIRLEY: Don't come near me!

LAURIE: It was you who came back! You didn't have to come! You
said you loved me! You said I made you feel a woman!

SHIRLEY: I didn't!

LAURIE: You did, you said it today, you said –

SHIRLEY: You don't think I meant it, do you? You don't think I meant
a bloody word of what I said to you! I hate you! I hated you touching
me! I wish you'd die! What do you think I wanted you for? For
baby, that's why, for my darling little girl who's never done a
bad thing in her life, that's why! That's why I let you touch me!
I wouldn't let you within a hundred miles of me otherwise! I've
never been unfaithful in my life, never! And I never will be! I think
you're dirt, is that clear? Dirt!

LAURIE (shattered): Yeah...

SHIRLEY: I don't ever want to set eyes on you again. Is that clear? I hope you're killed in an accident, I hope you die.

LAURIE: I see.

SHIRLEY (going out): And something else, too, just in case you've got any ideas - you were bloody hopeless. I was never so bored in all my life!

LAURIE: Right, okay then...

SHIRLEY: You're useless!

LAURIE (beginning to think he wants to be on his own): Look, just go, will you? Push off...

SHIRLEY (going towards him): All that for nothing, oh, Laurie, all that for nothing. And never before, I never did it before –

LAURIE: Get out, will you? Leave me alone and get out!

SHIRLEY: You've got to believe me, I'm not that kind of woman! Say you believe me!

LAURIE (thrusting her back by her shoulders): Get out! Fucking get out!

(He shoves her offstage.)

Out! Out! Out!

(The door slams. A long pause before he comes back into the room and collapses into a chair. He is still in a state of undress. He drinks from the bottle. He lies in this position for a long time, during which the lights fade to indicate late afternoon. BILL suddenly appears, and is astonished.)

BILL: What the hell –

LAURIE (leaping up, doing up his trousers etc.): Fuck off!

BILL (from outside the room): You're not one of them perverts, are you?

LAURIE: How the hell did you get in?

BILL: The door was open. I just came in.

LAURIE: How long have you been here?

BILL: Just came in. Just now.

(He re-enters.)

Is it something to do with a bottle? Is that part of it? I might be interested in that in the long lonely evenings.

LAURIE: You haven't been up to any voyeuring by any chance?

BILL: Was there anything to voyeur at?

LAURIE: If you want to know – I've had the perfect afternoon.

BILL: Oh, she was here, was she? Lucky cunt. I have to admit it, I envy you. You've got it made.

LAURIE: No, I haven't got it made. I made it myself. Nobody did it for me. All my own work.

BILL: Credit where it's due.

(He sits down.)

I was offered a job today.

LAURIE (bored): Oh, yes...

BILL: You're not interested?

LAURIE: Happens now and again, even to the best of us. You gave a thoroughly unfavourable impression, I hope?

BILL: Well...

LAURIE (turning on him): Well what?

BILL: Well, I was going to. And then... when I saw the place, I thought, well, it's got its advantages.

LAURIE: What bloody advantages?

BILL: Talent. Knicker. It was everywhere.

LAURIE: You didn't –

BILL: Not exactly.

LAURIE: Not exactly?

BILL: I have to confirm it tomorrow.

LAURIE: You're not –

BILL: I dunno!

LAURIE: You cunt!

BILL: Look, give us –

LAURIE: You cunt! What was it? It was the pension scheme, was it, the pension scheme grabbed you, did it?

BILL: Fuck off, Lol –

LAURIE: Non-contributory! That was what it was, that's what got your tiny mind working, the pension and the sports club!

BILL: The knicker!

LAURIE: No! Not the bloody knicker! What do you know about knicker? You wouldn't know what to do with it if it was free with cornflakes!

BILL: Get stuffed, Lol!

LAURIE: You bloody, fucking sell-out!

BILL: Only for the tarts!

LAURIE: You bloody liar!

(He walks to the window. A pause.)

BILL (meekly): Keep your hair on, Lol. You'll get a job yourself sooner or later.

LAURIE (turning): I will, will I? I'll get a fucking job, will I? You're telling me!

(Pause. He turns his back on BILL again.)

No, you never had it in you from the start –

BILL: No –

LAURIE: No, to be quite fair, you didn't. You never had it in you to be anything out the ordinary, I could see that from the start. You haven't got the cheek to make it big. Never will have.

BILL: Thanks a lot.

LAURIE: You get the job, it suits you. That's the life for you, taking your work home so you can get on in the office.

BILL: Very sarky.

LAURIE: You might make the junior grade if you do 'O' levels.

BILL: Look, I'm still with you –

LAURIE (facing BILL): No.

BILL: The property –

LAURIE: No. That's me. Just me. You get your job.

(Pause.)

BILL: All right, I won't take it.

LAURIE: You fucking will! Oh yes, you will. That's your cup of tea, that job is. You'll do very well in the social club, you will, with your habits. You might even make the Treasurer after ten years.

BILL: Look, no need to get –

LAURIE (conciliatory sarcasm): You're right, you're so right. No need to get het up.

BILL: We're still friends, aren't we? This isn't going to –

LAURIE: It won't make any difference. That'd be stupid, wouldn't it, losing a friend 'cos he's got a job?

BILL: You all right?

LAURIE: I'm perfect.

(Pause. They look at one another.)

BILL: You meant that, didn't you? About me being hopeless with women? You believe that?

LAURIE: I was annoyed.

BILL: You mean it?

LAURIE: I don't know.

BILL: Because –

LAURIE: Let's forget all about that, eh?

BILL (stifling a desire to prod further): Tell you what. I'll nip down and get a couple of pints, eh? Bring 'em back here?

LAURIE: Yeah.

BILL (going out): Five minutes.

(LAURIE stands about. There are a series of knocks on the ceiling. LAURIE takes no notice. They stop. The door slams.)

MUM: Laurie?

(Enters.)

Oh, you are in.

LAURIE: 'Course I'm in.

(He looks at her, surprised at her gay appearance.)

Home early, aren't you?

MUM (removing hat carefully): Oh, we had a half-day.

LAURIE: You've been drinking!

MUM: Only a few sherries!

LAURIE: You smell of it!

MUM (giggly): Do I? Really? I don't!

(She breathes into her hand.)

I do!

LAURIE: Nice party, was it?

MUM: Sir Geoffrey shook hands with everyone. He didn't miss a soul out.

LAURIE: That was nice of him.

MUM: You know, he said a few words to everyone.

(She sits down clumsily, knees apart.)

I think that's clever, don't you? The mark of a gentleman.

LAURIE: Definitely.

MUM: I mean, he couldn't have had anything to say to some people, but he still said it. I always say the Royal Family are good at that kind of thing.

LAURIE: What did he say to you, then?

MUM: Pleased to make your acquaintance. That was it.

LAURIE: Nice of him to say that.

MUM (smiling at the memory): It was, it was charming. Oh, he was a real –

LAURIE: You haven't asked me.

MUM: What?

LAURIE: About him. You always ask me about him. Why not today?

MUM: Well, only because you're so unpleasant.

LAURIE: Doesn't matter. You could ask.

MUM (surprised, naturally): Well...of course I want to know.

LAURIE: He's –

(Enter BILL with bottles.)

BILL: Drinks on me!

(He sees MUM.)

Oh!

MUM (smiling): You weren't expecting me!

BILL: No, I wasn't...I'll get you one, won't be a minute.

MUM: More drink!

BILL: What –

MUM: I've been drinking all the afternoon. Founder's Day. We call it Acorn Day, because that's our symbol. Sir Geoffrey said it's time we changed it to an oak tree. He was witty, you know what I mean? Always the right word.

LAURIE: I'll get you a drink.

MUM: That is nice of you, dear.

(Exit LAURIE. A pause.)

BILL: You look nice.

MUM: I do?

BILL: Certainly. You look – good.

(Pause. She smiles at him.)

I –

(Pause.)

What would you say if I said...I fancied you?

MUM: I'd say you were cheeky!

(She laughs.)

BILL: You must have thought about it...

MUM: Must I?

BILL: It's only natural. Women of your age...they have these thoughts about young men.

MUM: What thoughts?

BILL: You know what thoughts.

MUM: I do, do I? What can they be?

BILL: It must have crossed your mind. It must have. You're a good looking woman.

MUM: Oh?

BILL: Go on, deny it.

MUM: I –

BILL: You're blushing!

MUM: It's drink! It's all those sherries!

BILL: I know what you're thinking.

MUM: Oh, clever boy!

BILL: You think if I was to...to go up to you and go –

(He kisses her. She laughs.)

You wouldn't mind. You didn't mind, did you?

(He kisses her again.)

MUM: Well! You have got a nerve!

(He puts his hand under her skirt. The door slams. BILL stands up quickly. Enter LAURIE.)

LAURIE (slamming bottle down): Opener! Who's got the opener?

(BILL opens the bottles. They pour three glasses.)

Guinness for you –

(He hands a glass to his mother, but the party is interrupted by the banging on the ceiling. They all look up.)

Come on, drink up!

MUM: I'll go up.

(She stands up, totters slightly.)

Whoops! I'm not drunk! Isn't it terrible?

LAURIE (pushing her gently): You sit down, it'll go away if we ignore it, won't it?

MUM (in the chair again): What a way to talk!

LAURIE: It's not good for him to have his own way all the time, is it? He won't grow up properly.

MUM (laughs): No, I'll go.

LAURIE (preventing her getting up): We don't want to spoil him or he'll be a delinquent when he grows up. We don't want a delinquent, do we, Muriel?

MUM: I think he's –

LAURIE: Typical mother! Always sees the best in her baby. No, we'll sit this one out. We don't want the baby to rule our lives, do we? Babies have their place.

(Banging on the ceiling.)

MUM: He might be dying! Laurie –

LAURIE: Face down in his cot, you mean? No, wind more likely.

MUM (getting up): I'm going up!

LAURIE: Stay there!

(Pause.)

If someone's got to go, dada will. Dada will see to Baba.

(Exit LAURIE. His footsteps sound on stairs. BILL watches MUM, about to act, but her attention isn't there any more. After slower footsteps in descent, enter LAURIE, holding DAD in his arms.)

LAURIE: I've brought baba down.

MUM: Put him down!

LAURIE: He's sleeping, bless him. Ahh...

MUM (helping him put DAD in a chair): What did you bring him down for?

LAURIE: He was having nasty dreams, wasn't he? Did baba have a nasty nightmare then?

BILL: Is he all right? He looks a bit –

LAURIE (kneeling): All right? There's nothing wrong with our baby! Ugh! He's dribbling! Naughty, naughty! Wrap him up, Muriel.

(She pulls a blanket over him.)

MUM: He's not asleep, I saw his eyelids flicker. Supposing –

LAURIE (peering at the lop-sided head): Is he being deceitful? I don't want him growing up deceitful.

MUM: Leave him alone, Laurie –

LAURIE: You don't think his nappies –

MUM: The poor man! Help me pull him up straight, Bill, he's all tangled up in his dressing gown.

(BILL is a bit squeamish and manages to avoid actually touching him.)

There, that's better.

(She sits down.)

He can't be comfortable down here. It's not right.

LAURIE: He hates being left out of things, you know what he's like.

MUM: Look, his feet'll get cold!

LAURIE: Oh, I forgot his slippers! He loves his slippers, he's a right slipper merchant, is baba. Tell you what, we'll dust his feet and then put his slippers on. Where's the baby powder?

MUM (laughing now): Oh, Laurie, you are the limit!

LAURIE: We'll dust his horny little feet and then we'll put his toggy woggy slippers on. I'll get them, don't worry, I'll get them. I'll get his toggers!

(Goes off. MUM smiles at BILL, and BILL goes over to her, puts his hand on her breast and kisses her.)

MUM: There's a time and place!

(They kiss again. Enter LAURIE.)

LAURIE: Where's the baby powder?

(BILL is stunned. MUM tries to smile but fails.)

I said where's the fucking baby powder?

(The silence continues. LAURIE goes to DAD and lifts up his head.)

He didn't see it. He was looking the other way. He missed it, he missed the whole bloody lot! Here –

(He jerks DAD's head round.)

Carry on, now he can see, go on, get on with it! Go on, down with 'em, take your bloody pants down. What are you waiting for!

MUM (not very successfully): I'm not going to be insulted by you.

LAURIE: You set a very bad example, don't you? I was hardly out the door. My back was hardly turned! Baba might have seen it! He might have seen his mumsa being dirty with his dad's best friend! What would he grow up like! Have you thought of that! Have you? Have you thought of that, you dirty bitch?

MUM (getting up): Here, I've had enough –

(LAURIE pushes her back into the chair.)

LAURIE: Sit down!

MUM (getting up again): I won't!

LAURIE (pushing her back): You will!

MUM (to BILL): Are you going to let him –

LAURIE: Him? Him do anything? Oh, fuck me!

MUM: You dirty-minded little bastard!

LAURIE: In front of your own baby! You bloody bag!

MUM: I'm not going to be insulted by you.

BILL: I think I'll go.

MUM: I'll come with you!

(They start to leave.)

LAURIE: Go on! Get up some bloody alleyway! Hey! Did you know she had varicose veins? Did you know that?

(MUM slings a glass of beer over LAURIE. It silences him.)

MUM: You bloody little drowned rat!

(After a moment, the lovers go off. LAURIE remains stunned for some moments, then he goes a little way off as if going after them.)

LAURIE: Here, we were going to have a good time, you and me! Eat out for a change!

(After a pause, he enters, hesitates, then goes off in the opposite direction, returning with a towel with which he wipes his hair. When he's finished, he exits, goes upstairs, and there follows the sound of drawers being opened and flung about. All the time DAD sits drooping in the middle stage. Eventually LAURIE comes down with a heavy case, jammed with MUM's clothes. He flings it on the floor, and sits down, exhausted, staring at the floor. After a few moments, he notices a pair of her knickers. He takes them out of the case, and examines them. Then he notices his father. He places the knickers on his father's head.)

You saw all that, did you? Out the corner of your eye? Of course, you wouldn't know what it meant. I mean, you're just a baba. If you saw his hand up her skirt, you wouldn't know what he was doing, would you? You wouldn't think he had his fingers up her fanny, would you? It's funny, but I came out of there. In the afternoon, it was. Out I came, sliding onto the table – bump! Wheeeee – bump! Funny that. Funny fanny. Fannies are funny! Fun in the funny fanny!

(Pause.)

I bet she had to squeeze though. She's got such little hips. I expect those officers put their finger up her fanny. What a history her fanny's got. Not that you care, eh? I can see you don't care. I'm the only one who's actually lived in there, actually been in all the way, head and shoulders. I expect you wish you could. But you're too big.

(Pause.)

She messed us about, didn't she, baba? I had it all planned, what we were going to do. And then she did that to us. Poor baba. Now it's just me and you, eh? Just baba and Dada? Eh?

(Pause.)

Look at that sun. It's sunny now. Shall I take you in the yard? You want to? You like that, eh? I wish you were a bit more talkative, you don't say much. Here, say something, any old thing, even if it's only boo!

(Pause.)

You are difficult. You haven't died, have you? Have you? You wouldn't admit it if you had, you poor bugger. Come on, let's go.

(LAURIE picks DAD up and carries him out. His voice is heard outside the empty room from the yard.)

Is that all right? See the sunsa shining? And all the little birdies? Say boo to the birdies, go on, say boo. Say boo! Say boo!

THE END

Number Three

John Grillo

Number Three was first presented at the Soho Lunchtime Theatre
Club on June 16 1970, with the following cast:

NUMBER THREE   Henry Woolf
NURSE   John Grillo

Directed by Frederick Proud
Assisted by Paolo Lurati

Very loud music, lights flash on to show THREE who is seated on a
chair in the middle of the stage. There is a very neatly made bed in
one corner. The walls are white or grey. Down stage there is a door.

THREE: Churchillian. Yeomanlike. Solid. Chinny. Stalwart and
    stubborn. The last British tommy. Irremovable. They may ad-
    vance on me with coshes, hypodermic syringes, and fists full of
    ten shilling pieces but I will be irremovable. The bed is there and
    I am here and that is how we stay.

    (Enter NURSE.)

NURSE: Good evening, Three.

THREE: Good evening, Nurse.

NURSE: Time for bed, Three. I suggest you slip out of your garments,
    draw yourself into your pyjamas and get ready to drift away on
    the raft of sleep into Nod land.

    (Aside.)

    You may say, why talk to the poor lunatic as if he were a baby?
    My answer to that is he doesn't understand a word I say because
    he lives in a world of fantasy. I sympathize with him but I can't
    waste my time talking to him.

    (To THREE.)

    Come along, Three, take your clothes off and get into bed.

THREE: Piss off. Piss off. Piss off.

NURSE: Not four-lettered words again. How very boring.

    (Aside.)

I know some people get excited by four-lettered words such as piss, cock, fuck, arse or cunt. I'm a normal man myself and never go to the theatre because I enjoy watching television on my nights off but I understand that whenever a four-lettered word is uttered in the theatre, one section of the audience stands up and cheers, while another section walks out very red in the face. In the lunatic asylum you get these words thrown at you all the time as if they were bombs.

THREE: Piss off. Piss off. Piss off.

NURSE: Three, I have the feeling you are going to be difficult tonight.

THREE: Piss off. Piss off. Piss off.

NURSE: What's the matter, Three?

THREE: I refuse to go to bed. I refuse to go to bed. I have decided to declare myself England and you Germany. Therefore why should England go to bed at Germany's bidding? Englishmen are free. Piss off. Piss off. Piss off, cries free England at the Teutonic invader.

NURSE: Why won't you go to bed, Three?

THREE (after a pause): That would be telling.

NURSE: Are you frightened?

THREE: Of course not. Englishmen are brave.

NURSE: Three, unless you undress and get into bed, I'll report you.

THREE: Why are you so anxious to see me naked, Nurse? Is it because I've got such a beautiful body and you are a voyeur?

NURSE: Unless you undress and get into bed, you will be punished.

(THREE laughs at him.)

THREE: Voyeur, you want to look at me naked, probably when I'm on the toilet.

NURSE (aside): It's very frustrating because I'm a normal man with a normal urge to put the boot in. I'm training my son to play for Chelsea and imitate the heroic deeds of Captain 'Chopper' Harris! In ancient lunatic asylums Wardens, as they were called instead of Nurses, were supplied as part of their medical equipment with black jacks and bother boots. The incidence of cure was much higher than it is now. I might raise that at the union meeting.

THREE: Talking to yourself again, Nurse?

NURSE: Shut up, Three, I'm thinking.

THREE: Thinking about putting the boot in and beating me on the head with the bed pan no doubt. Drop the idea, Buster, because I've got influence in high places. The Governor of the asylum is married to my sister, Miss Ermentroyd. He got her pregnant in a punt because he refuses to use a sheath. Now I know it's only coloureds don't use sheaths because they are proud of their sperms and like the woman to feel them splodge like a cannon shot against the back wall of the womb. So by putting two and two together I discovered the Governor's secret - he's a negro.

NURSE (aside): You see how horrible it is in a lunatic asylum?

(To THREE.)

Three, you have dirty minded ideas. You know very well the Governor is a white-skinned bachelor. He is a true English gentle-man who would never infiltrate a woman without first asking per-mission and he always wears a cricket blazer and a sheath.

(Aside.)

I hope he heard that. I don't want the sack.

THREE (shouting): The Governor is coloured and the Nurse is a voyeur. I'm the only sane one here and I'm refusing to go to bed.

NURSE (aside): Sometimes I get furious with Three for inventing these dirty fantasies but I have to restrain myself and be circum-spect or I'd lose my job and the wife and family would starve.

THREE: You are a very inferior man, Nurse, working for a Governor who's coloured.

NURSE: Tell me, Three, why are you frightened of going to bed?

(There is a pause.)

Well?

THREE: You'll laugh at me if I tell. You'll call me a fibber.

NURSE: No I won't, Three, I promise you.

THREE: Very well then. It's a well known fact that I'm a genius on a par with Jesus Christ, Eddison and Lord Montgomery. You are of course familiar with that fact?

(There is a pause.)

Well?

NURSE: Oohm.

THREE: Come here, Nurse. Closer because I want to whisper in your ear the true reason why I refuse to go to bed.

(The NURSE comes closer.)

Murder is a terrible thing, Nurse, and so is sexual relations with negroes. The genius cannot walk among inferior men without arousing their ire and spite. The inferior men I refer to are your fellow nurses. The negro I refer to is the Governor of the asylum who because of the colour of his skin is more interested in sex than in running a lunatic asylum. He'd far rather stick his cock up Ermentroyd's fanny than take my temperature and I have a very beautiful temperature.

NURSE (aside): What a dirty crack. He really is disgusting.

THREE: The genius I refer to is myself. I persuaded the Governor it would be better for all concerned if he retired and made me heir to the Governorship of the asylum...

NURSE: How?

THREE: I blackmailed him of course, you stupid oaf. Really if you can't show more acumen you'll be the first man fired when I take over. The Governor and I drew up a secret contract. However, the nurses discovered...

NURSE: How?

THREE: The lawyer blabbed. Not to worry though. He got his deserts and his body is now floating under Hungerford Bridge... in six pieces. People who ask awkward questions often find the same sort of thing happens to them too. The nurses, disturbed that a lunatic should be put in charge of the asylum, formed a cabal and swore an oath to murder me. However, the nurses are cowards which is proved by two facts: firstly only cowards work for negroes and secondly all murderers are cowards. They know I have the strength of ten men...

NURSE: Three, it's a myth that lunatics have the strength of ten men.

THREE (after a pause): I know it's a myth, Nurse, but firstly the Nurses don't know it's a myth and secondly it happens to be true in my case. I do twenty or thirty... hundred press-ups before breakfast. And unlike the Governor I'm more interested in the size of my biceps than in the size of my cock.

NURSE (aside): Another dirty crack about the Governor. My fear is that the Governor will see through an intercom system these dirty cracks being made and will see me not doing anything about it and will sack me. On the other hand we're forbidden to put the boot in. It's a dilemma.

THREE (shouting): Therefore the reason I refuse to go to bed is because the beds in this asylum are soft and my flesh is soft and I would fall asleep and a crew of fiends would creep into my room armed with chair legs, bread knives, cleavers, wood choppers, coshes, hypodermics, iron bars, razor blades, scissors, forks, socks full of sand, electric wires and old bones. Nobody would come to my aid, not even my sister, because she never leaves the Governor's lush apartments but sits all day in a negligée on a sofa drinking tea and varnishing her nails. This crew of fiends I refer to are the yellow-bellied, chicken-hearted, jelly-boned, quivering, shaking, defecating in terror, smelly, bullying nurses of this asylum.

NURSE: Three, it infuriates me to hear the nursing profession maligned by the lips of a lunatic. Nurses are not yellow-bellied, chicken-hearted, jelly-boned, quivering, shaking, defecating in terror, smelly bullies, they are an underpaid underfed overworked, philanthropic, altruistic, sweet and excessively kind band of champion charmers.

THREE: I beg to differ.

NURSE (aside): I could kick him. I could even bite him. I really could.

THREE (standing on a chair and shouting): I am the Governor's heir and a genius. Your Governor is a negro and the nurses are thuggish.

NURSE (aside): We call that delusions of grandeur mixed with persecution complex. The two always go together... like love and marriage.

(Nicely.)

Nobody wants to hurt you, Three, you are safe here.

(Aside.)

That's not strictly true because I want to bite him but I'll keep control of my self.

(Nicely.)

Come down off the chair, Three. Who knows, you might fall off and break a leg. Your leg would be in plaster for months and all the lunatics would laugh at you as you hobbled around. You don't want that do you?

(Aside.)

It's no use appealing to reason, I shall have to assert myself.

(Loudly.)

Come down off that chair immediately, you lunatic.

THREE: Piss off. Piss off. Piss off.

(A voice off calls NURSE NURSE.)

NURSE: That is Number Seven, Three. Number Seven is a good boy. I shall go and kiss the good boy good night. When I come back I want the bad boy in his pyjamas.

(Aside.)

While I'm away I'll consult Dr Rommell's Book of Nursing Ethics. I'll think up some tactics.

(To THREE.)

You look very stupid up there.

THREE: Piss off. Piss off. Piss off.

NURSE: It's disgusting.

(He goes away.)

THREE: The bed is there and I am here and that is how we stay.
Churchillian. Irremovable. He didn't believe me. He wasn't taken
in. I must reconsider my tactics.

(Enter the NURSE.)

NURSE: What a good boy Number Seven is, Three, I had no time to
say Jack Robinson before he jumped into bed.

(Aside.)

Also in the time I've been away I've read Dr Rommell's book from
fly leaf to index. He has some brilliant tactical suggestions.

THREE (looking up): Sex.

(He looks down.)

NURSE: What?

(NURSE sits down on the bed. He puts his head in his hands.)

Poor Nurse is worried because Number Three is such a bad boy.
Nurse is a very sensitive man and he cries when Number Three
plays him up. Nurse begins to think that perhaps Number Three
doesn't like him or has no respect for him, when he says naughty
things about the Governor and the other Nurses. Poor poor Nurse
cries because Number Three won't go to bed.

(He begins to cry loudly. He stops. To the audience.)

This is called 'Making the patient feel guilty'.

(He starts crying again.)

Poor poor Nurse crying his heart out because naughty Number
Three won't come down off the chair and get into his pyjamas.

(Slowly NUMBER THREE gets down off the chair. He goes over to
the NURSE and pats him. He looks at the NURSE. NURSE looks at
him.)

Poor Nurse.

THREE (aside): He's been reading Dr Rommell's Book of Nursing
Ethics again.

(He sits down next to the NURSE.)

There there, Nurse, no need to cry.

(Aside.)

The silly bugger.

(To NURSE.)

I'll strip off my shirt and trousers and pop into my pyjamas.

NURSE: Thank you, Three, you are a good boy at heart.

(Aside.)

Thanks to Dr Rommell's instant remedy for recalcitrant patients.

(THREE stands up and begins to unbutton his shirt. The NURSE stands up.)

I'll help you, Three, because you are such a good boy.

THREE: Thank you, Nurse.

(The NURSE takes the shirt off.)

Oh, it feels like I'm being peeled. Being undressed by you has always been my day dream, Nurse.

NURSE: Take your trousers off, please.

THREE: You are keen, aren't you? Will you unbutton them for me?

NURSE: Unbutton them yourself, Three, that's what fingers are for.

THREE: I thought fingers were for something else.

NURSE: I don't follow your line of argument.

(Aside.)

What's he on about.

THREE: There's no need to be shy with me, Nurse, I understand your sort and I reciprocate.

(He unbuttons the trousers slowly and they fall to the floor. He steps out of them. He wears Union Jack underpants. He strolls over to the chair and stands on it as before.)

Here I am, Nurse, naked as nature intended and you've always wanted.

NURSE: What?

THREE: Nurse, the real reason I refuse to go to bed is that I want to stroke and kiss you all night long and you want to stroke and kiss me.

NURSE: Rubbish. Nonsense.

(Aside.)

That's a complete lie. I only hope the Governor is not listening in on the intercom system. He runs a very moral asylum.

THREE: I love you, my darling, my sweetheart, and you love me. I want to kiss your lovely face all over and hug you in my arms. I want to kiss your belly button and tug the hair on your chest.

NURSE: Not even my wife knows about the hair on my chest, Three, it's a subject that never crops up in decent conversation.

THREE: You are a notorious queer, Nurse, but there's no need to be ashamed because I'm queer too.

NURSE: I'm heterosexual, Three, and what is more I'm disgusted.

THREE: Aren't I pretty enough for you, Nurse? Only yesterday the Governor said to Ermentroyd 'Your brother is the most pretty lunatic in the asylum'. And he should know because he's a negro.

NURSE: The Governor is not a negro. He would never allow a phrase like that to pass his lips and he is not married to your sister.

THREE: I'm willowy, Nurse. I'll sway if you'll give me a puff of wind. I've got a slender waist and my skin is white as snow. I've got two little brown nipples and lips like strawberries. My eyes are as blue as the summer sky and my things are soft and squeezable. A soft and squeezable me, Nurse, soft and squeezable.

NURSE (aside): I'd like to assure you that I'm not in the teeniest bit aroused by this list of so called charms. I train my son to put his cock in wherever he finds it. My reaction is normal. I'm nauseated that a human being can sink so low.

THREE: You spy on Number Seven when he's sitting nude on the toilet doing his business.

NURSE (aside): Where does he get these ideas from?

THREE: You make Number Twelve lie face down on the bed nude and you stick your finger up his bottom.

NURSE (aside): I regard the sole function of the human bottom as defecatory. It is not for me an erotically stimulating zone.

THREE: Number Six told me you ordered him to piddle into your mouth even though there was a potty in the room.

NURSE (aside): The emotions I am feeling now are anger at being falsely accused, frustration at not being able to vent my anger, fear that the Governor may hear these accusations and get the wrong impression and horror on a philosophic level that a human being could have such perverse ideas. I sometimes wonder if he isn't a man from Mars.

THREE: I saw you carrying a pair of black leather boots this morning.

NURSE: Three, I was polishing those boots for the Governor who likes to go riding.

THREE: What about the truncheon in your belt?

NURSE: That truncheon is for ultimate use on recalcitrant patients and you are rapidly becoming one.

THREE (shouting): Nurse is queer, a flagellant and an experimenter in sexual perversion.

(To NURSE.)

It's all right though because I'm an experimenter in sexual per-version and won't report you. Shall I make a long list of the things you can do to me?

NURSE (aside): I think we are just about to have a demonstration of the reason that he is a lunatic and I am a nurse.

THREE: Use me and abuse me after your own fashion, Nurse. Lick my bottom and suck my cock... for a start. Tickle my bottom while wearing a nylon stocking over your head. Smell the aroma of my socks. Suck my feet while I'm wearing a rubber macintosh. Make me eat your faeces which you carry to me in a cornflakes bowl. Make little nicks in my cock with your razor blade and lick the blood. Clip off my pubic hair with a pair of scissors and eat it. Stick your cock up either of the two orifices in my body while I've got my hands tied behind my back. Get a saw and saw my arms and legs off and take photographs of the mutilated corpse. Put my meat in a pot and cook me and eat me. I'm all yours.

NURSE (aside): Although Number Three has interesting complications, his basic problem is that he's obsessed with sex.

THREE: So you see, Nurse, the reason I refuse to go to bed is that I want us to do things together. Do you want me to take my under-pants off?

NURSE (aside): Dr Rommell, you met your Waterloo. What am I supposed to do when confronted with this lavatory? He makes me want to vomit. When he makes suggestions like that I want to throw up the dinner that my lovely wife spent hours over a hot stove cooking right in his face.

THREE: Do you want me to take my underpants off?

NURSE: No, Three, that won't be necessary. As a special treat you can get into bed with them on.

THREE: Will you join me?

NURSE (assertively): No, Three, I'm not going to join you in bed. Get that through your thick lunatic skull. I'm going back to my wife and family.

(Aside.)

My wife is a lovely woman. She doesn't know the sort of work I do because it would worry her. You see it was the only job I could get after I left the army.

(Shouts.)

I'm not going to join you in bed. Get that through your thick lunatic skull. I'm going back to my wife and family.

(Aside.)

A peck on the cheek when I go through the door. Slippers by the coal fire. Pipe on the mantelpiece. Dinner piping hot in the oven. Plenty of spuds. Television in the corner. Kids doing homework. Wife knitting socks. The poetry of home.

(Shouts.)

I'm not going to join you in bed. Get that through your thick lunatic skull. I'm going back to my wife and family.

THREE: Are you playing hard to get?

NURSE (shouting): No.

THREE (aside): I think I misinterpreted the situation.

(To NURSE.)

Would you repeat that, please?

NURSE (shouting): I'm not going to join you in bed. Get that through your thick lunatic skull. I'm going back to my wife and family.

THREE: I didn't think you'd be able to resist me when I was wearing my underpants. I thought I looked like Martine Carole.

(Pause.)

I think sexual perversion should be severely punished, Nurse. Queers should have a red hot poker driven up their bottoms. On the other hand that might give them too much pleasure so perhaps they should just be hanged.

(Pause.)

You're not queer, Nurse, but all the other nurses are. The Governor is queer. He married Ermentroyd because she resembles me. He tried to seduce me by walking about in his underwear but because I've got similar feelings as you I rejected him out of hand. We could be brothers, Nurse. So he married her instead. There are two reasons I refuse to go to bed. Firstly the nurses all love me and like the idea of raping me and so if I put my pyjamas on and get between the sheets they will all rush in en masse and rape me. Secondly the nurses all hate me because they are jealous of the queer grip I have on the Governor whose arse-lickers they are and so if I put on my pyjamas and get into bed they will all rush in en masse and kill me. Therefore, Nurse, it's your duty as an anti-queer to let me stay up.

(Pause.)

What do you say, eh?

NURSE (loudly and clearly): Piss off. Piss off. Piss off. I'm going, Three, and if you are not in bed when I come back I shall use the ultimate weapon.

(Aside.)

Dr Rommell, I'm swapping you over for the Wellington boot. Bolder tactics are called for.

(He goes out.)

THREE: Churchillian. Irremovable. Solid. The bed is there and I am here and this is how we stay. Armageddon draws nigh.

(Enter the NURSE. He looks determined and carries a large truncheon. He addresses the audience.)

NURSE: This is what we call the ultimate weapon.

THREE (aside): It's what they call the ultimate weapon.

NURSE (aside): When a lunatic sets his eyes on this he starts to shake with terror.

THREE (aside): Not shaking.

NURSE (aside): He squeals in desperation.

THREE (aside): Not squealing.

NURSE (aside): He starts to sweat.

THREE (aside): Not sweating.

NURSE (aside): He dribbles like a baby.

THREE (aside): Not dribbling.

NURSE (aside): He defecates in his underwear.

THREE (aside): Not defecating.

NURSE (aside): The reason that the ultimate weapon is so seldom used is that the nurses have to clean up afterwards.

(To THREE.)

Number Three, get into bed, or I shall use the ultimate weapon on your head. This is Armageddon.

THREE: This is Armageddon, Nurse.

NURSE: This is Armageddon, Three.

THREE (approaching the NURSE): If you strike me with that truncheon, Nurse, you will suffer. Remember that I am Number Three, the genius on a par with Jesus Christ, Eddison and Lord Montgomery. I am the Governor's happy favourite lover and a backstairs influence via my sister Ermentroyd.

NURSE (raising the truncheon above his head): I'm raising the truncheon into striking posture. The day of argument is over.

THREE (very arrogantly): I've got the strength of ten men and your
stupid truncheon will break on my head. I'm more interested in
the hardness of my head than the hardness of my cock.

(He walks round the NURSE who himself turns so he always faces
THREE. Like a Samurai.)

The Governor is hiding under the bed and he is my lover. He will
hold you down in a zinc bath and I will stand over the bath and
piddle into it until you are up to your neck in piddle and then the
Governor will hold you under until you either drink your way out or
drown.

NURSE: Prepare yourself to be struck, Three.

THREE (screaming): You will look stupid as the Governor holds you
under the piddle. All the lunatics will laugh at you as you drink
the piddle.

NURSE: Your threats don't hold water, Three, you live in a world of
fantasy.

THREE (screaming): I will bury you, I will bury you.

NURSE: The truncheon will be descending soon, Three, you have one
last chance to give yourself up. You know you're done for.

THREE (screaming): Piss off. Piss off. Piss off.

(NURSE hits THREE on the head with the truncheon. He falls flat
on his face.)

NURSE: You saw I gave him his chance to come in quietly but he had
to resist. You can't do a thing with them when they are in that
guerillarish mood.

(He pulls THREE onto the bed and puts him under the sheets.)

I won't take his underpants off as somebody might get the wrong
impression. Go to Nod land, Three, and let's hope you show a changed
face in the morning.

(He goes to the door.)

A peck on the cheek when I go through the door. Slippers by the coal
fire. Pipe on the mantelpiece. Dinner piping hot in the oven. Plenty
of spuds. Television in the corner. Kids doing homework. Wife
knitting socks. The poetry of home.

(He goes out of the door. NUMBER THREE speaks in a very deep
voice. He is still unconscious.)

THREE: Churchillian. Irremovable.

(Blackout and loud music.)

There's No Point in Arguing the Toss

Don Haworth

There's No Point in Arguing the Toss was first broadcast on the BBC Third Programme on April 6 1967 with the following cast:

GEORGE	Derrick Gilbert
FRED	James Bolam
SMITH	David Mahlowe
IRISHMAN)	
SECOND BUS CONDUCTOR)	James Beck
FRED'S MUM)	
TURNSTILE WOMAN)	Barbara Greenhalgh
GATEMAN)	
CROCKET)	Colin Edwynn
JONES)	
MAN)	Jack Woolgar
INSPECTOR)	
FIRST BUS CONDUCTOR)	Geoffrey Banks
HARRIS)	
FAIRGROUND ATTENDANT)	Frank Marlborough
WOMAN	Ruth Holden

Produced by Alan Ayckbourn at Leeds Studios

Laughter of a mechanical laughing clown. Other fairground sounds. The laughing clown again. Shrieks, groans, laughter of the ghost train. The sound of its cars. More remotely, other fairground sounds.

GEORGE: Of course after the event everybody's very wise and fruity about what you should have done and what you shouldn't have done. We shouldn't have let our dad go on the ghost train. We take the point. But he wasn't what you'd call a nervous type and I've never heard before of anybody being frightened to death. I mean literally frightened to death. He must have been dead the first time round, but me and our Fred were some distance away chatting up some birds and we just thought he was staying on for another ride. It's funny the attendant didn't spot it because at that rate you could have people paying a shilling and riding round and round all day. Anyway the next time round we were up by the rails and the attendant was a bit more on his toes.

ATTENDANT: There's a gentleman here's passed on–

GEORGE: – the attendant said.

FRED: He's our dad –

GEORGE: – our Fred said.

ATTENDANT: I extend my personal sympathy but the company holds itself in no way responsible for loss, damage, injury or accident, however incurred.

FRED: All right, all right.

ATTENDANT: It's displayed there and printed on the back of the ticket.

FRED: He can't read, he's dead. And we don't want to argue the toss.

ATTENDANT: There's no toss to be argued. I extend my personal sympathy without prejudice to the fact that the company holds itself in no way responsible.

FRED: All right. Let's get round to him.

ATTENDANT: You can't come through the turnstile without paying. It registers and it's checked against the cash.

FRED: How much?

TURNSTILE WOMAN: Is there two of you? Two shillings.

(Money is put down. Turnstile clicks.)

ATTENDANT: There's nothing in the form of a platform ticket here so if you pass through the turnstile at all you've got to pay the full price for a ride.

FRED: We'll forego the privilege. We just want to get him home.

ATTENDANT: He'll have to go in the accident book.

FRED: It's not an accident, man, he's dead.

ATTENDANT: We don't keep a death book. Accidents include death but deaths don't include accidents.

FRED: It's not necessarily so either way.

ATTENDANT: There are people waiting for a ride. It's neither the time nor the place for a barrack room lawyer.

FRED: We're not barrack room lawyers. We're the next of kin of the deceased.

ATTENDANT: Are you saying that those propositions are mutually exclusive?

FRED: We're not saying anything. We don't want to argue the toss.

GEORGE: But that's exactly what they were doing – our Fred and the attendant – arguing the toss, and the car set off again before anybody could press the button or whatever stops it, and our dad went sailing round for another lap.

(From the ghost train whoops, shrieks, laughter.)

It's pretty macabre stuff having a real live corpse riding round on the ghost train – or rather a real dead corpse – and I suppose comical if you're that way inclined, but me and our Fred felt ridiculous standing there on the platform and by the time he came round again a fair old crowd had collected at the rail.

FRED: Disperse –

GEORGE: – our Fred said, but they didn't seem to understand the word. He rephrased it with two short words they did understand, and immediately there was a hullabaloo.

(Protests from the crowd.)

WOMAN: He worked for you when you were little, didn't he? And you using language in front of his mortal remains.

MAN: With ladies present.

WOMAN: To say nothing of ladies being present. It's a very unsavoury incident.

GEORGE: They went on chewing the rag and the attendant insisted on putting our dad's particulars down in his goddamned book, then some Mick at the back of the crowd felt the time ripe to make himself heard.

IRISHMAN: He's in need of a priest.

WOMAN: Or a clergyman of some kind or another.

MAN: Denomination.

WOMAN: A man of God of one description or another.

MAN: Denomination. That's the correct word in this context.

FRED: Thanks, but he never went in for that kind of thing.

WOMAN: That's his loss. This is exactly the kind of situation where you need the consolation of religious faith.

FRED: All right, all right.

MAN: You've got to believe in the hereafter and reunion with loved ones. You can't just think he's had his chips, that's his lot. Life would become meaningless.

IRISHMAN: Shouldn't the police be summoned?

MAN: You can summon them but they won't come. They're all en route for the football match. There are none left to deal with untoward incidents in other parts of the city.

FRED: It's not an untoward incident. He's passed on. It comes to us all. George, take his weight on your shoulder.

GEORGE: And our Fred lifted him gently and with such care that they suddenly went quiet and I couldn't see them anyway for tears and I can't remember anything till we got to the gate though we must have walked half a mile humping him through the sideshows, being stared at in passing by people who probably thought nothing more about it. The gateman was a fat little bloke with war medal ribbons and he launched out in a reasonably sympathetic manner.

GATEMAN: Hard luck. How did he cop it?

FRED: On the ghost train.

GATEMAN: You never know which one has your number on it, as it says in the Good Book. Hard luck.

GEORGE: And he fished out his key to open the big double gates they let charabanc parties in through.

FRED: No ostentation, please. We'll go through the little gate for pedestrians.

GATEMAN: He's not a pedestrian.

FRED: He's not a coach party either. We don't want to argue the toss.

GATEMAN: You'll wear his boot toes out humping him along like that.

FRED: Are they your boots?

GATEMAN: I'm not saying –

FRED: Well, belt up then.

GEORGE: And it was on this acrimonious note that we left the amusement park and went to wait for the bus. You might think that in the circumstances we'd have gone in for a bit of private transport, a taxi or perhaps given a van driver a quid to whip him home. But the point is we'd always come out together on the bus with Red Rover tickets and we'd always gone home together on the bus. It was a habit that we'd all joined in and it would have been letting him down to have abruptly discontinued the programme just because he'd passed on. You hear old birds at a funeral when they get maudlin say 'He'd have liked that'. What the thing is is neither here nor there. They mean that they're carrying on at something regardless, same as if the deceased wasn't deceased. I'm not saying it's victory over death or any of that crap but it does make folk less of a complete goner if you take the trouble to persist in what they'd have been doing if they hadn't snuffed it. If that's too involved for you, never mind. I'm just explaining why we went on the bus. Now what follows is about bus conductors and I know it is bound to stir up the dirt with the Transport and General Workers' Union. The fact remains that a certain percentage of bus conductors are rotten. You see a woman, say, with two kiddies and a fold-up pram struggling to get into the bus and they not only leave her to it but make her all flushed and embarrassed by standing there looking impatient with their thumb on the bell. I'm not saying all conductors, but the fact is they just don't get officer material on the buses. The hours and wages are simply not conducive.

(Bus approaches.)

GEORGE: First it was the 72X.

(Bus stops.)

1st CONDUCTOR: No drunks.

FRED: He's not drunk, he's dead.

CONDUCTOR: The same rule applies.

FRED: What rule?

CONDUCTOR: The management reserve the right of admission.

FRED: That doesn't apply to the buses.

CONDUCTOR: It does apply to the buses.

FRED: Where is it stated?

CONDUCTOR: I'm stating it.

FRED: He has the right to travel on the bus.

CONDUCTOR: The only people that have the right to travel on any bus is the people that hold tickets for the journey in question.

FRED: Right, that's us. We all have Red Rovers.

CONDUCTOR: Use them on the next bus. We've already been overtaken by the 72 that's three behind us. Get a taxi.

(Bell rings and bus goes off.)

GEORGE: Anything in fact but take a bit of responsibility himself. That's what I meant about not getting officer material on the buses. Missing this 72X put us in a predicament because the best bet then was the 104, which went into the centre where the football specials waited and there was already a long queue for it, football supporters with scarves and rattles and toppers and whatnot.

(Queue sings 'Ee-aye-addy-ho we're going to win the cup'. Rattles sound.)

It had come on raining a bit and we weren't going to hump our dad to the end of the queue. At the same time it wasn't right for us to muscle in at the top and given a situation of this kind and people in a Saturday afternoon mood you can't calmly negotiate at what point of the queue you ought to enter it as a special privilege in the circumstances. So we stood at the top of the queue and there was a certain amount of chunnering which is understandable. People at the bottom of the queue craned forward to see what was going on and an argument broke out some distance down the line when we took the weight off our shoulders a bit by propping our dad against the bus stop.

SMITH: Was he en route for the match?

FRED: No, he'd been on the ghost train.

SMITH: He didn't miss his bit of pleasure then.

FRED: No.

SMITH: You know, it occurred after rather than before. At a big
match, say, a lot get carried out even before the teams appear so
they have all the trouble of getting dolled up and changing buses
and perhaps buying a programme and then not being spared to
witness the event alluded to in the programme. Sometimes they've
a hell of a job to get the programme out of their grasp.

FRED: It could have happened a lot worse.

SMITH: He'd had his ride.

FRED: He got three for the price of one.

SMITH: Fair enough. And he'd had his Saturday dinner.

FRED: No. Our mum works Saturday mornings. We just have a bit of
breaky, then we come out with a Red Rover and tour up and down,
then my mum has a decent blow-out ready for us when we get back.

SMITH: And that's been a ritual, like?

FRED: Every Saturday since our George could walk. Well, I'm saying
every Saturday but only within reason. Not if it's pissing down.

SMITH: There's no point in getting soaked.

FRED: Or if we have folk coming to the house.

SMITH: You've stuck together as a family.

FRED: Correct. Some blokes are same as lodgers. In for meals then
cheerio till bedtime. Some blokes you see them trailing round
shopping with birds with rollers in their hair, looking at furniture
and all that. Anything but go out with their own family.

SMITH: Have a snout.

FRED: Don't smoke, thanks.

SMITH: Did he smoke?

FRED: No.

SMITH: See, you can renounce all worldly pleasures, then it comes
like that.

FRED: Being a non-smoker doesn't necessarily make him into a saint.

SMITH: No, but the point remains... You could call an ambulance.

FRED: No thanks.

SMITH: It costs nothing. Just threepence for the call.

FRED: We'll go on the bus.

SMITH: Or you could dial 999 and have it entirely buckshee.

FRED: That's not the point. The point is that we've come out together every Saturday.

SMITH (sympathetically): Bar when it was pissing down or you had folks coming.

FRED: And we've been round together on the Red Rover to lots of places – places that lots of folks in this city don't know about even though they're living on top of them – and we've gone home together. Way things has turned out this is the last jaunt and we owe it to him to take him home in a normal decent manner on the bus.

SMITH: Fair enough. I admire you for it. If more young fellows had your sentiments we wouldn't have all these unofficial strikes to contend with...or the balance of payments...or all these immigrants coming in reducing the value of property. I'll put a word in for you.

FRED: We're against racial discrimination.

SMITH: All the same.

(Shouts.)

Listen...listen...Hold that rattle still, son...Listen. There's a gentleman here had an accident so let's not have the usual stampede please when the bus draws up.

JONES (distant): What's up with him?

SMITH (shouting): He's had an accident.

JONES: Has he passed out?

SMITH (shouting): On or over rather than out.

HARRIS: Should get an ambulance.

JONES: Call a taxi.

SMITH (shouting): And his son here wishes to take him home on the bus in the normal manner. So no stampeding, please.

(Speaks.)

You'll be all right. I was a respected member of the Ladybrook Brass Band for seventeen years.

(Sound of bus approaches.)

SMITH (shouts): All right, it's coming. It's not an electric hare so don't bound out of the trap.

(Bus stops. Queue surges.)

Hold it, hold it.

CONDUCTOR: Upstairs, all of you.

SMITH: Right, conductor. There's a gentleman here passed on.

CONDUCTOR: Hump him upstairs.

FRED: He's a non-smoker.

CONDUCTOR: Look, it's a concession to let him on at all in that state. The upper saloon, please. We've already...

FRED: I know.

CONDUCTOR: You know what?

FRED: You've already been overtaken by the bus that's two behind.

CONDUCTOR: A bit fly, eh? This isn't a hearse, you know. You can take your pick - upstairs or wait for the next bus.

HARRIS: Come on. Get on with it.

SMITH: Hold it, hold it. Give him air.

HARRIS: What's he want air for?

SMITH: He wants respect.

HARRIS: You said air.

SMITH: Look, I was in the Ladybrook Brass Band for seventeen years.

GEORGE: Well, the repartee continued at roughly this level with a certain amount of jostling and pushing and the conductor standing there impatient with his thumb on the bell, as I mentioned before, until our Fred took hold of our dad under the arms and started to struggle backwards upstairs with him.

(He struggles up the stairs.)

FRED: Guide his feet, George.

GEORGE: And there was something about the way he lifted our dad that made them all go quiet - same as with the crowd when he humped him out of the ghost train. It was the expression on his face like you see on madonnas in art galleries. Quiet - reposeful rather. Dedicated. Those are the words. As if there was nobody within a mile of us. I could see them all pushing and gawping and having their bits of arguments in the mirror when we went round the bend on the stairs. Our Fred couldn't see the mirror because he was backing up, but even if he could he wouldn't have looked into it because all his heart was in getting our dad upstairs and you would have thought he was deaf for all the notice he took of the stir we created on the upper deck.

CROCKER: Is that a corpse you've got there?

GEORGE: He simply didn't hear. Some uncouth merchant damn nearly legged him up with a dog lead, shifting hastily with his dog,

like they were doing - dogs or no dogs - to the seats at the front.
Our Fred simply didn't notice. He plonked our dad down by the
window and sat beside him and nodded me into the seat in front.

(Bell rings. Bus moves off.)

The man who had been in the brass band parked himself beside me.

SMITH: They're a good lot, United supporters. You can always rely
on them to act in a restraintful manner in a case of this sort. They'd
sing a hymn if I asked them.

FRED: Thanks, but we'll take it as read.

SMITH: No, seriously. They all know 'Abide With Me'.

(Shouts.)

You all know 'Abide With Me'.

(Speaks.)

They sing it at the Cup Final.

GEORGE: And he took a lad's rattle and began to conduct.

SMITH (singing): Abide With Me, fast falls the eventide...

OTHER VOICES (joining in increasingly): The darkness deepens. Lord
with me abide.
When other helpers fail and comforts flee
Help of the helpless, O abide with me

SMITH (alone): I need they presence every passing hour.

(He continues unconfidently beneath narration.)

GEORGE: But the rest of them didn't know the words of the second
verse and the man from the brass band was left warbling on his
tod till our Fred brought the axe down on the proceedings.

FRED: All right. That'll do. You've made your point. Thank you.

GEORGE: The man from the brass band motioned to them to fill up
the seats round us. They had left a kind of cordon sanitaire round
us which could have made us feel conspicuous but, fair play to the
sods, they did move in upon request and this confirmed the man
from the band in the role he'd taken upon himself as our handler or
impresario or PRO or something.

SMITH: These lads have been telling me they've been out with their
dad here every Saturday, come hell or high water, bar when it's
literally pissing down or they have folks coming. I'll bet if you
added it all up he's clocked a fair old mileage riding round on the
ghost train.

FRED: We haven't come here all that often.

SMITH: See, living opposite the amusement park I don't think I've been inside it since I took my sister's kiddie on and he's an insurance agent now.

HARRIS (to the boys): Where did you go then?

SMITH: I'm making the point that, living on the doorstep, you get blasé, though they come in charabanc loads from miles away, Yorkshire, all sorts of damn queer places.

HARRIS: Where did you go then besides the fun fair?

(Pause.)

JONES: The lad doesn't want to talk.

FRED: It's not that. Put baldly like that it's hard to remember. Museums and places.

HARRIS: Art galleries?

FRED: Like in one museum there's a tree made out of stone fossil – dating back to the Ice Age.

HARRIS: There were no trees in the Ice Age.

FRED: There was this tree because it's in the museum.

HARRIS: Not in the Ice Age.

FRED: If you want an argument you'd better go and argue with the curator.

HARRIS: There was nothing grew in the Ice Age. It was all just ice as the name infers, entirely barren.

JONES: The lad doesn't want to haggle about fossils at a time like this.

FRED: It's not that, I just haven't got the background. The little picture - plaque is it? - at the bottom said it grew in the Ice Age. I'm only telling you what the plaque said. I wasn't there.

SMITH: It'll be a shock to your mum. Was he in the war?

FRED: He was on munitions He never did anything. He drifted in and out of jobs and on the public assistance, but he was the life and soul of everything. Everybody knew him for miles round. He was pleased with everything just like a little kid. Same as with this tree. He had no background either but he'd have put it better than me.

HARRIS: It couldn't have grown in the Ice Age.

FRED: Well, you say that to me and I think, all right, get stuffed. But my dad had a way with him. He'd agree with folk whatever they said but they'd finish up agreeing with him. That doesn't make sense, does it?

GEORGE: I don't think our Fred had ever spoken two consecutive sentences about our dad before. It was amazing seeing him sitting there by our dad holding forth glibly on all manner of topics.

JONES: I understand. He was a charming man. A gentleman.

FRED: Outside the house.

JONES: He was a good dad to you.

FRED: He was rotten at home.

SMITH: You're upset, lad.

CONDUCTOR: Any more fares please.

GEORGE: Our Fred held the three Red Rovers up without thinking
about it and he went on talking regardless of the audience, the
same as he'd humped our dad up the stairs heedless of people
peering and boggling, and they were shuffling about in their seats
and you could see they felt the time ripe to drop the subject but
once he'd got under way it just didn't occur to our Fred that it was
unsuitable to ventilate his thoughts on private matters to a load of
football supporters sitting on top of a bus with our dad cooling off.

SMITH: 'Treat every man according to his deserts and who would
'scape a whipping?' as Wordsworth said.

FRED: That's not the point.

SMITH: The point is you're inferring he was strict with you. He
probably conceived it his duty. But on your own admission he's been
romping round town with you every Saturday, bar certain honourable
exceptions, seeing a bit of life.

FRED: And a bit of death now.

SMITH: Today's an exception. It's none of my business but I don't see
what you're holding against him.

FRED: All right. I don't want to argue the toss.

SMITH: You'll feel better when you get home.

FRED: It won't alter the record.

SMITH: You'll feel different about it when you get older.

FRED: What I feel isn't the point. It's just a sad dismal record for
him to have to live with.

GEORGE: Well, there was a pause. You could see the point registering
even on the thickest of those present that our dad didn't have to
live with his record. That is just what he didn't have to do, having
passed on. You could see the brass band man wanted to do whatever was kindest, to let the subject drop or give our Fred a sympathetic hearing, whichever was for the best. He made a couple
of false starts then said.

SMITH: Is it a police record, like, you're alluding to?

FRED: No, he had no police record. I mean the neighbours called the
police dozens of times but we weren't taken down to the station
for a hammering or hauled in front of a judge or anything like that.
Domestics – the police just don't want to know. All right, they'd
say, we don't want to know but cut out scrapping round the happy
home. It upsets the old ladies next door.

SMITH: Who was scrapping then?

FRED: Me and my dad. Our George here had a few bouts with him
but usually me and my dad.

SMITH: And it rattled the old ladies next door?

FRED: Next door but one actually. Next door the poor sod's deaf so
it didn't worry him.

SMITH: He was impervious to bumping and banging.

FRED: That's it, bumping and banging. He'd throw anything. He's
smashed everything in the house that could be thrown.

SMITH: He was handy with the furniture then?

FRED: Stools and chairs mainly. He'd ram you up against the wall
with the table, then hurl anything he could lay his hands to. He'd
have you fixed like a clay pipe in a shooting gallery and he'd just
cob everything.

SMITH: Was he always like that?

FRED: No, when I was little he just used his fists but once I started
fighting back – when I was fifteen or so – I realised he was careless
with his right elbow. He carried it high, you know, not tucked in,
so I thought right I'll stop him with one in the guts. It knocked the
wind out of him. You'd have thought a balloon had been let down.
He was still unsteady on his pins next morning.

SMITH: And you rue it now, belting your dad?

FRED: Yes, I rued it and he rued it, but it didn't stop us from sailing
in next time. See, our George here with being the youngest hasn't
had nearly the same amount of fighting in the home. I think he
thought we enjoyed it, you know, did it for fun. My mum's brothers
would come round and the police and they'd all say be reasonable,
cut out the scrapping round the happy home. But he couldn't help
it because he'd always thumped me and once I'd put him down for
the count I understood exactly how he felt. You think how awful and
after all he's done for me and you get so screwed up that you've
just got to belt him again.

SMITH: Did you never really get on with him?

FRED: I wouldn't be sitting here with him now if I didn't get on with
him.

JONES: Human relationships are never simple.

SMITH: Fair point. It's just that it's not usual to elaborate to a bus load of strangers.

FRED: Well, isn't it? I mean how often have you travelled on a bus with a corpse and his relatives?

SMITH: No, it just seems a bit clinical trotting out his weak points and him just passed on.

FRED: Passing on doesn't make him a saint. A lot of people pass on but only a few of them get registered as saints.

JONES: I'm on your side. You want to take him home in a normal way on the bus and you don't want him lost in encomium or eulogy.

FRED: What's that?

JONES: The old geguffle. We shall not see his like again and all that crap. I remember when we put my uncle up the chimney they got in a proper qualified reverend, C of E I think, and he launched into a eulogistic description of my uncle that damn near annihilated the poor old bastard's memory. He used to dope dogs.

SMITH: You're not saying this gentleman here was a dog doper?

JONES: Who said I was saying he was a dog doper?

SMITH: You made an allusion.

JONES: To my own uncle.

SMITH: Your dad didn't dope dogs, did he?

FRED: No.

SMITH (to JONES): Are you convinced?

JONES: I take his word. The point is –

SMITH: Fair enough then. Dog doping doesn't enter into this gentleman's record in any shape or form. You're out of order.

JONES: I'm not out of order. You were saying why bring up all the dirt and I'm giving you my answer. This lad obviously loves his dad and he doesn't want the memory of him lost under a load of hypocrisy. His dad's all right to him exactly as he was, faults and all.

SMITH: But he wasn't a dog doper. Agreed he was a bit rough about the house but there's no question of doping dogs. It's not germane.

JONES: All right. All right. He did well for you in many directions, didn't he?

FRED: I can't think of any off hand, but that's damn all to do with whether you love somebody or not, hasn't it? He mucked everything up.

JONES: Not everything surely. He knocked the premises about a bit, but you've grown up strong and reasonably educated.

FRED: I'm not reasonably educated. As I said I've got no background.
If some bloke says trees didn't grow in the Ice Age –

HARRIS: They didn't. Entirely barren –

FRED: I haven't got the background to argue the toss.

JONES: Whose fault is that?

FRED: Same as with busting up the happy home, mine and his between
us. Funny thing, we had a 'Home, sweet home' thing done in fretwork, craftsmanship and all that, that hung on the wall. He splintered it over my head.

SMITH: A bit symbolical like.

FRED: That's the point. The 'sweet' was cracked right across, being
in the middle, so for a lark our George here cut it out and stuck the
ends together so it said 'home home' and you can see the mark like
on the wall from where it used to be longer. My mum christened
it 'Home, home on the range'.

SMITH: I know, I know.

(Sings.)

Home, home on the range.

OTHERS (joining in increasingly):
Where the deer and the antelope play
Where seldom is heard
A discouraging word
And the skies are not cloudy all day.

(General applause. Sound of rattles. CONDUCTOR pounds upstairs.)

CONDUCTOR: Cut it out. No more singing.

SMITH: You can't enforce that, conductor.

CONDUCTOR: Behaving in a riotous manner. There's ladies downstairs.

VOICE: Send 'em up then.

(General assent and laughter.)

CONDUCTOR: I've let you bring your corpse on, but don't push it or
we'll end up driving round to Lloyd George Road police station.

(Cries of dissent and abuse.)

I've told you. We did it a couple of weeks ago. We'll do it again.
Grown men!

(More dissent and abuse. CONDUCTOR clumps downstairs.)

JONES: I wasn't here. What happened?

HARRIS: We was late for the match.

SMITH: They pulled up outside Lloyd George Road Police Station and the bobbies came out in their braces and sorted a few hooligans out.

CROCKER: What do you mean hooligans? My brother was amongst those remanded in custody.

SMITH: They were all young lads.

CROCKER: That doesn't make 'em hooligans. He's earning £18 a week on a lathe.

HARRIS: It doesn't follow. My brother worked a lathe but he finished up marrying a woman out of a circus.

CROCKER: What's that got to do with it?

HARRIS: He worked a lathe but his artistic inclinations put him on wrong lines notwithstanding.

CROCKER: My brother has no artistic inclinations.

HARRIS: Well my brother had. He'd sit down for hours on end and play novenas on his shillalagh.

CROCKER: Aaaar, he's half way round.

HARRIS: I'll be down there in a minute.

(CONDUCTOR has clumped upstairs.)

CONDUCTOR: Did you not hear what I said about driving round to Lloyd George Road Police Station?

(Silence.)

All right then, watch it. This bringing a corpse on public transport is going to be reported anyway.

(Silence. He clumps down.)

JONES (to be kind and preoccupy FRED's attention): What was that then you was saying about your education being neglected?

FRED: I didn't pass my eleven plus, that's all.

JONES: You think a more stable home, so to speak, would have made the difference?

FRED: It wasn't that. In his own way he was trying to help me. Like he was very glib and top of the morning and all the rest of it outside the home, but inside we never had what you might call close con- versations. You know, I used to think when we were out and he had everybody laughing and really interested himself in all sorts of things, you know, I used to think if only I could have him like that to myself. But once we got over the threshold he said virtually bugger all. Like a comedian. You meet him in private life off the stage and he's just like anybody else. He has to have an audience to come alive.

JONES: And that affected your education.

FRED: No, well like as an exception to saying damn all, he gave me
a bit of an address, a long speech really, my mother had put him
up to it, when I was doing my eleven plus. He kept drying up and
he didn't know where to look but he stuck at it and ploughed on ad
infinitum.

JONES: It's understandable. He might have been a bit garrulous –

FRED: What's that?

JONES: Went rabbiting on.

FRED: That's what I'm saying.

JONES: But he was trying to give you the benefit of his experience.

FRED: I'm not denying that. The point is what he was on about. He
intended it just to be encouraging but he went on about how he was
a failure and he didn't have no opportunities and what did I think
he felt when other fathers could take their children away on holi-
days, humping their luggage to the bus stop and some of them
bowling away in secondhand cars, you know one owner, careful old
lady, then you find it's been used in a bank robbery.

SMITH: I'm getting a bit lost.

JONES: The thread was that his brief address put you off your stroke.

FRED: It wasn't brief, but he said: 'Look, Fred, don't be a layabout
like me. Pass this here examination and make a man of yourself.'
I was eleven years old at the time.

JONES: What's wrong with that?

FRED: As you said yourself it put me off my stroke. I hadn't done no
homework. The telly's on all the time and you can't get on the
table when he's in. He's always brewing up and cooking himself
an egg or something.

JONES (kindly): You won't have that trouble any more...I shouldn't
have said that; it was tactless.

FRED: It's quite true. But that wasn't the point. See, if I'd have passed
he'd have gone round crowing to people. 'Our Fred's passed for
the grammar school' and, say on Saturdays, he'd have had me
dolled up in grammar school gear telling the museum curator and
the ghost train bloke and whatnot 'Our Fred's at the grammar
school studying Latin and pyrotechnics and God knows what'.

JONES: He'd have a right to be proud of you.

FRED: That's what I thought. He thumps me round the happy home or
he sits there brewing up and saying bugger all, then he wants me
to perform at the eleven plus to give his own pride a bit of a face

lift.

JONES: There's another side to it.

FRED: I'm coming to it. It's not like consistent with what I said. In fact it's the opposite but nevertheless it applies. I pitched up for the exam at the stated time and a little bloke with a ginger moustache starts laying down the law. 'Don't turn the question paper over till I fire the gun. Don't speak to your neighbour. Don't write in the left-hand margin. Don't do this, don't do that, don't breathe.' So I thought, Sod 'em. There was something queer about the classroom. I don't mean the desks being in single file and the floor being swept clean for once and this little bloke with the ginger moustache not being our regular teacher. So I let him rant on - I'd no option anyway - and I tried to figure out what it was, you know, queer. Well, it was right in front of me. I could see it all the time, but it startled me. All the blackboards were absolutely blank. There wasn't a word on any of them. So I said to myself, 'Who says my dad's a layabout? Who the hell are they to sit and pass judgment?', and this little ginger bloke said in his educated way 'You may now commence' and I thought 'Sod 'em. They can get stuffed' and I didn't write a word all morning.

JONES: You made no attempt whatsoever?

FRED: I did actually. I didn't have the courage of my convictions. Like this little ginger bloke kept craning round and peering at me sitting there and then he came up leaning on me, mumble, mumble, mumble, and all bad breath. Then he took me outside and began making the point, and he said he'd report me to the Minister of Education or somebody and I thought we'd have the police round again and a delegation of my mum's brothers laying down the law to my dad. So I wrote my name and did one or two sums, but it was eleven o'clock before I done a stroke.

JONES: And your dad was disappointed?

FRED: No, he never asked me. He knew I'd fail. Like I went home screwed up to tell him because I never went in for telling lies. But he never asked me. He went and brewed up and he said, 'Have a cuppa, Fred', which was something unusual because he usually drained the teapot on his tod. We sat there saying bugger all and swigging tea and it was right grand for both of us - I can't describe it - and he said 'Let 'em get stuffed', and I thought about this little educated ginger bloke poncing about in front of his bare blackboards and it was right grand sitting there boozing tea with my dad.

(Sound of bus running.)

GEORGE: They didn't say anything. They just nodded, at first in sympathy and then with the motion of the bus, nodding, nodding, nodding, all the way to the city centre and our Fred didn't seem aware of anybody at all once he'd finished his discourse.

(Bus stops.)

SMITH: All right, we're here. Volunteers, please, to help get this gentleman down the stairs.

(Passengers get out and go downstairs.)

GEORGE: Of course most of them made a mad rush for it but the blokes we had been talking to stayed behind to help and so did the pasty youth whose brother had been among the hooligans the police sorted out on the bus a fortnight ago. He was wearing a striped football topper. Our Fred made a gesture to them meaning thanks but stand clear and he lifted our dad gently and carried him down the stairs.

(FRED descends. Sound of traffic and football crowd in city centre.)

GEORGE: The problem then was how to get on a bus at all because the football specials fill up rapdily. You have to run to the back of a queue that winds round the town hall. One bus goes and another comes in and it's every man for himself. The four blokes who were helping us stood round in a quandary. You wouldn't believe it but nobody in all those thousands in the city centre took a blind bit of notice.

SMITH: Look we can't fight 'em and we can't join 'em. We'd better get a taxi.

FRED: The bus is the way he'd expect to go home.

(Silence.)

JONES: Hang on. I'll get the inspector.

GEORGE: The inspector looked over at us when the man told him, then he went along the line of buses, standing on his tiptoes, shouting in to the drivers. God knows what for because you'd think it would be simple enough to fill up and drive to the football ground, but I suppose it's what he was paid for and a dozen buses had come and gone before our acquaintance got him over to us.

INSPECTOR (breezily): What's your game?

FRED: We don't have a game, he's died.

INSPECTOR: This is pretty sick stuff, isn't it, taking a corpse to a football match? Are you from Candid Camera?

FRED: We want to go home.

INSPECTOR: Where's home?

FRED: Longshaw Lane.

INSPECTOR: Where did you start from?

FRED: Home.

INSPECTOR: And you're going home? Home from home.

GEORGE: Well, of course it raised a laugh because we were all thinking of the fretwork motto our dad had splintered over Fred's head and 'Home, home on the range' like they'd sung, but the inspector took it as a tribute to comic genius and it cost us nothing to let him go on thinking that.

INSPECTOR: Look lads, I've got my hands full keeping the buses on the move. This isn't a publicity stunt, is it?

FRED: Death needs no publicity.

INSPECTOR: Where did you start from - not home but this last journey?

FRED: The amusement park.

INSPECTOR: And it's not publicity?

FRED: Look, have you ever lugged your own dad round dead?

INSPECTOR: I mean your connection with the amusement park.

SMITH: There's confusion here. They were customers at the park not employees. This gentleman passed on on the ghost train.

INSPECTOR: Call an ambulance.

SMITH: They don't want an ambulance. They want him to finish in a normal decent way on the bus.

INSPECTOR: You should have got the 72X. It had have dropped you off at the bottom of Longshaw Lane.

FRED: We know all that. We don't want to argue the toss about it.

INSPECTOR: Are them Red Rovers you've got in your hand? You know you can't use them on the football buses. In any case you'd want to get out at Pole Road, wouldn't you, and the football buses don't stop while they get to the ground.

SMITH: Get us a bus and we'll give you a quid.

GEORGE: Well, that put the matter in an entirely different light and he was back at the other side of the square shouting on his tiptoes into a cab window and the driver looked across and wrestled with his wheel and the bus pulled out of the line and rolled round empty to where we were standing.

SMITH: Quick, get him in.

GEORGE: We just made it. There was a hell of an uproar in the crowd and they swarmed across shoving the police horses aside up the town hall steps, grabbing the rail, pulling their pals on board as the bus gathered speed, leaping some of them and missing and rolling in the road. You'd have thought it was D-Day. And they went on arguing the toss and shouting till the conductor stopped the bus for us at Pole Road. It was only then when we were getting him down

that they realised there was a deceased person on board. The
blokes who had helped us got off with us.

FRED: Don't trouble yourself further. You'll miss the match.

SMITH: We'll give you a hand, son. I'm only sorry it wasn't done with
more decorum.

FRED: We'd sooner hump him ourself if you don't mind. Take his
feet, George.

GEORGE: Well, they hesitated a bit, then they followed a few yards
behind, three middle-aged men in football scarves and the pasty
youth in the striped topper. At one stage we stopped for a rest and
there was a great explosive roar from the football ground.

(The roar is heard.)

The teams must just have come out. These blokes were obviously
a bit wistful about missing it but they didn't show it. They stood at
a respectful distance, ready to give us a hand if we wanted it, but
our Fred didn't and they just followed up in case. Our Fred stopped
short of our door.

FRED: I'm wondering how's the best way to put it to her?

GEORGE: But he didn't want an answer from me and the blokes
realised he didn't want suggestions from them either. He stood
holding our dad up against the wall, and you could see how much
they looked like each other and our Fred simply didn't know where
he was or what to do and we'd have been standing there yet if the
brass band man hadn't stepped forward. Our Fred waved him off
and did it himself, not having thought it out, in the worst possible
way.

(FRED knocks on door which is opened.)

MOTHER: Fred, what's happened? What's happened, Fred? Who are
these men?

GEORGE: They were standing a few yards away and the brass band
man gave the pasty youth a dig and glanced at his striped topper.
The pasty youth doffed it and held it in front of his chest like a
promenade Percy in a Victorian portrait.

MOTHER: Fred. Your dad, Fred. What's happened?

FRED: He's a goner.

MOTHER: But Fred, I've got his Saturday dinner ready.

FRED: Let's get him in. Lift his feet, George.

GEORGE: And we got him in and laid him out on the couch and without
thinking my mum closed the door and we never said thanks to the
blokes or offered them a cuppa or even gave the man his quid
back.

MOTHER: But Fred, how can he, Fred? I've got his Saturday dinner ready. It's in the oven, roast lamb. I've got his Saturday dinner ready.

GEORGE: And she went on and on and the room was bare of ornaments which our dad had flung at Fred and the 'Home home' sign that had been a bit of a joke for us was up on the mantelpiece with the mark on the wallpaper behind, and nothing seemed any different from any Saturday. Our Fred could have said something to please her or explain things like he had on the bus. But he didn't. He just sat there like our dad used to do in the happy home as though he didn't care a damn about anything.

FRED: All right, mum. There's no point in arguing the toss.

Superman

Pip Simmons Theatre Group

Dedicated to President Nixon and Screamin' Jay Hawkins 'whose efforts to recapture the era of the early '50's do not pass unnoticed'.

INTRODUCTION

This is not a play script in the conventional sense but a record of a play which started out with one idea and during the course of 250 performances and some cast changes came to a number of different conclusions about its dramatic pretensions. It is probably more useful to consider it as a scenario - written after the play was performed and very near to its phasing out of our repertoire.

During the one and a half years in which we have worked on the play (we have constantly re-rehearsed and revised it) we have performed mostly to 'educated' audiences and this has somewhat dictated, due to the necessity of being able to live, how the play has evolved in terms of clarity and 'entertainment' emphasis. We in any case came to the decision that Superman was a nightmare for some, an intellectual, irresolvable jig-saw puzzle for others, and mostly a satirical entertainment which 'went a bit further'.

For us the play was an attempt to investigate our own attitude towards theatre, to create for the group a way of performing which would recognize its own limitations and make those limitations, although attempting to alleviate them, a starting point for group creation.

We chose Superman partly for the theatrical possibilities it offered and partly because of our nostalgia for the period in which we all first discovered the live energy in performance of the 'rock'n'roll' era. The performance is an attempt to recreate the crudity, vulgarity and excitement of the times and also to impose our own 'profound' judgement on the horrific monster that was emerging in the shape of 'middle class liberal morality'.

Superman, despite the London critics' dubiousness, is a myth; not in the traditional sense but in the modern idiom; he is a media myth, a film star, an idol, a joke; everything one associates with our cynical attitude towards concepts that get out of control. He is the bastion of the 'American Dream'.

It was not our intention to provide a working script but to suggest possibilities to a group with five months spare time. The technical problems of staging, costume (we used American football gear), lighting, will find their own answers.

Superman is a comic strip play whose chief source is an actual comic strip story called 'Rock'n'Roll Superman'. Some of the additional material (and we have plagiarized and borrowed unscrupulously) is from literary sources; however, the style of playing implied by comic strip should be applied at all points so that the final product has as its basis a carefully explained sequence of events involving a collection of colourful, but in every case, two-dimensional characters, who should by virtue of their uncompromising heroism or villainy, cleverness or stupidity, courage or timidity, be able to wield the same power over their audience as the comic strip characters wield over most of their readers - by no means all children.

Superman was first presented by the Pip Simmons Theatre Group at the Mickery Theatre, Loenersloot, Amsterdam on May 11, 1970 with the following cast:

Ben Bazell
Glynis Earl/Lu Jeffery
Warren Hooper as Superman
Paddy O'Hagan
Annie Eills/Sue Watson
Chris Jordan
Eric Loeb

Directed by Pip Simmons
Music by Chris Jordan

SINGER:
>   Metropolis: sorrows beyond telling;
>   Sickness rife and foul, outstripping invention of remedy -
>   Blight on barren earth and barren agonies of birth.
>
>   Life after life from the fiery riot swinging
>   Swiftly into the night beyond all telling.
>   Metropolis reeks with the death in her streets death-bringing.
>
>   None weeps, none weeps and her children die. (repeat)
>   None by, none by to pity.
>   Man of steel, man of steel, come near to our crying.
>   Man of steel, night's agony grows into tortured days;
>   The thunders crash and the lightning slays.
>   Man of steel,
>   Man of steel...
>   From the grim reeking death...comes a figure.

(The CHORUS enters at the end of the above song - sung as a lamented blues - and speak their lines in strict rhythm to the accompaniment of a typical rock beat. The rhythm should be used by them to generate the kind of enthusiasm which the call and response rock songs used to generate in the '50's. In a simple dance the CHORUS underline and emphasize their words with strong gestures communicating strength, speed etc.)

CHORUS:
Faster than the speed of light...
Stronger than any man alive...
Able to leap tall buildings...
Is it a plane?
Is it a train?
NO........
It's Superman!

SINGER:
Faster than the speed of light
Stronger than any man in sight
Able to leap to any height
The only thing that turns him off is kryptonite...
All right...all right...
Is it a plane? Is it a train? No, it's Superman!

SUPERMAN: Ohmiiigosh! All I can do is rock'n'roll when I hear that music; it's...it's...it's uncanny.

SINGER:
With his super breath and his super brain
He foils the crooks again and again.
He can see through their plans, he can see through their lies,
He can see through brick walls with his X-ray eyes...

FANS:
Cool Superman
You're a super-cat
Dig that crazy rhythm.
Great Superman, great
Super bobby-soxers.

SINGER:
What the...? Who the...? How the...? Wham!
Whoosh. Zoom. Boom. Bam.
Splat. Zap. Zonk. Pow.
Oufff. Ouch. Aagh. Eyow.
All right etc.

SUPERMAN: Ohmiiigosh!

FANS:
Superman is always cool.
Cool, cool, super-cool.

SINGER:
Cool, cool, super-cool
. . . .
He's cool
He's cool
He's cool. Cool. Super-cool.
He's a super-cat.

(The above scene is the equivalent of the comic strip trailer frame – the large picture at the beginning of each story which anticipates the particular dangers that Superman will face in the ensuing tale. The function of this first frame is to attract the reader's attention.

The song and the interjections of SUPERMAN are in a straightforward rock style and rhythm. The song begins slowly in order to make SUPERMAN's accompanying dance, which again reflects the sense of what is being said, as deliberate and clear as possible; speeding it up as it progresses so that by the last chorus, it has reached a frenzied pitch in rhythm and voice.

The next sequence of CHORUS lines is the final introduction to the story and should combine the naive admiration of a child for his comic hero, the self-interested enthusiasm of a lunatic ad-man for his product and the reverence of the philosopher for 'the ultimate man'.)

CHORUS (speaking individually in turn):
This is the time.
This is the famed hour.
The fabulous moment.
Time for the death slayer.
Behold I will show you the ultimate man.

ALL:
Woweeeeee!

INDIVIDUALLY:
Behold I give you the Superman.
Superman is...the meaning of the earth.
Superman shall be...the meaning of the earth.
Today we bring you a tale when...
The world's most fabulous hero
The greatest adventure character
The famed flying figure
The man of steel becomes...
Where is the lightning to lick you with its tongue?
Where is the madness with which you should be cleansed?

SINGER: Behold I give you the rock'n'roll Superman.

ALL:
He is this lightning.
He is this madness.

WOWEEEEEEEEEEEE!

SUPERMAN: This is a dream...

CHORUS: This is a dream...

(The members of the CHORUS repeat the sentence or sections at random as if asleep; one by one performing various manifestations of their dreams e.g. neurotic, agonized, verbose etc. SUPERMAN performs keep-fit exercises. Eventually the phrase 'meet Jimmy Olsen', spoken first by one voice then taken up by all, emerges from the dream sequence and begins the next scene.

This should be played at great speed but with the emphasis on explaining to the audience in a patronising way the finer points of the plot. The CHORUS, which can be split as indicated in the script, assists this explanation both by making their own comments (2) and by prompting JIMMY and the MANAGER (1).)

FIRST CHORUS SPEAKER: Meet Jimmy Olsen, cub reporter for the Daily Planet and friend of Superman.

ALL: WOW!

JIMMY (reading the newspaper): WOW! Rock'n'Rollsen's in town. Why, that's my cousin Jerry Olsen. I haven't seen him since we were at college together. I'll kill two birds with one stone when I interview him for the Daily Planet at his hotel. WOW! I'll bet he's happy with all his fame and fortune as a Rock'n'Roll singing star.

FIRST CHORUS SPEAKER: But just how wrong can Jimmy be...

SECOND CHORUS SPEAKER:
Fame brings much fun and publicity
but also heavy responsibility.
See now the dilemma facing Jerry Olsen as Jimmy meets his manager.

JIMMY (arriving through Jerry's MANAGER's door): So where's Jerry then?

MANAGER: The kid's got the chicken pox, Jimmy. It looks like we're gonna have to cancel all the concerts in Metropolis.

(Two bars of 'Money' on the piano.)

JIMMY: Aw, shucks. Just think how disappointed all them kids'll be.

MANAGER: I know, Jimmy, we sure don't want to let them down.

JIMMY: I just wish there was something I could do to help.

FIRST CHORUS SPEAKER: Suddenly Jerry Olsen's manager has a brainwave.

MANAGER: Hey.

(No brainwave.)

SECOND CHORUS SPEAKER: Jimmy looks like Jerry...Jimmy looks

like Jerry...

MANAGER: Jimmy looks like Jerry. Hey, kid... maybe you can help at that. You're a dead ringer for Jerry... and that gives me a humdinger of an idea.

(Puts false wig etc. on JIMMY.)

Now with these on you can pass for Jerry on stage...

JIMMY: WOW! On stage...

MANAGER: And take his place...

JIMMY: WOW! Oh that this too solid flesh would melt etc...

(MANAGER exudes enthusiasm for JIMMY's performance.)

FIRST CHORUS SPEAKER: As Rock'n'Rollsen... as Rock'n'Rollsen...

MANAGER: As Rock'n'Rollsen!

FIRST CHORUS SPEAKER: But surely Jimmy can't sing like Jerry.

JIMMY: But holy cow! I can't sing like Jerry.

SECOND CHORUS SPEAKER: But Jerry's manager has all the answers.

MANAGER: That's no problem... Jimmy.

(He hasn't a clue.)

FIRST CHORUS SPEAKER: Mini tape recording... mini-tape-recording...

MANAGER: Use this mini tape-recording of all Jerry's songs and play them back through the mini-recorder inside Rock'n'Rollsen's guitar. Jerry used it when he had a sore throat.

JIMMY (confused): So I...

FIRST CHORUS SPEAKER: Pretend to strum and sing.

JIMMY: So I...

FIRST CHORUS SPEAKER: Pretend to strum and sing.

JIMMY: So I... Hey!

(Conspiratorially.)

So I pretend to strum and sing so that all the kids'll think I'm Rock'n'Rollsen.

MANAGER: That's about the size of it kid. O.K. Whaddya say?

JIMMY (cutely): O.K. I'm game.

SECOND CHORUS SPEAKER: So plucky Jimmy practises hard for an hour miming and gyrating to the music...

MANAGER: Now listen to this, kid, I want you to repeat after me: the best things in life are free...

(JIMMY repeats it flatly and monotonously.)

But you can give them to the birds and bees.

(JIMMY repeats it as before.)

The best things...

(JIMMY repeats it more enthusiastically.)

In life...

(JIMMY repeats.)

Are free...

(JIMMY repeats.)

You can give them...

(JIMMY repeats.)

To the birds...

(JIMMY repeats.)

And bees.

(JIMMY repeats.)

ALL: WOW.

SECOND CHORUS SPEAKER: Until...

(The following should be frenetic and intense: JIMMY singing wildly out of tune; the MANAGER throwing money in the air draws the chorus into his fantasy. They mob him leaving him with his trousers round his ankles. Everybody sings 'Money' according to their own particular fantastic involvements in the sequence.)

MANAGER: Say, that was great kid; even I can't tell the difference...

(He pulls up his trousers.)

...so I'm sure the kids won't.

FIRST CHORUS SPEAKER: What about the boss?

JIMMY: O.K. I'll just ring my boss and get some time off.

MANAGER: Fine. But don't tell a soul why...

(Very loud.)

If this ever got out...

FIRST AND SECOND CHORUS SPEAKERS: Shhhhhhhhhhhhhhhhhhhhhhh!

MANAGER: Jerry might lose all his fans...

(ALL whisper anxiously to the audience...communicating the calamity directly. Next CHORUS line emerges from this whispering.)

SECOND CHORUS SPEAKER: Meanwhile back at the theatre in
Metropolis...

CONNIE SKUNK (singing the archetypal Frankie Lymon and the
Teenagers late '50's ballad...accompanied by close harmony
vocal backing...'ooh-wahdy-wahdy, chum-dooey-dooey');
Each time we have a quarrel,
It almost breaks my heart,
Because I'm so afraid
That we'll have to part.
Each night I ask the stars up above...
Why must I be a teenager in love

(Last line ad infinitum.)

COMPERE (interrupting CONNIE's prolonged and overdone final note
with appreciation both professional and patronising): Thank you
Connie Skunk...and now what I know you've all been waiting for...

(The fans scream dementedly.)

...now is the hour...

(Screams.)

...here he is cats....that teenage singing sensation...Rock'n'
Rollsen.

(Screams.)

(JIMMY jumps into position and freezes with COMPERE into cartoon
frame of the moment. The FANS take up the CHORUS and take up
positions as participants in the TV discussion. Associations with
normal TV discussions need not impose a static style on the scene.
Using the idea of how these cardboard personalities speak, one has
ready-made cartoon self-parodies: they perform a dance which reflects the particular manner of their speaking.

The CHAIRMAN is neutral; only more so. CON GEEL is one of
pop music's intellectuals: his movement is a literal representation
of his inability to take more than two intellectual steps forward
without taking at least one backward. PHYLLIS's forcefulness and
verbosity suggest a series of expansive and athletic gestures whilst
ANGELA's mindless affectations are reserved much more for a
British fringe socialite. Alternately, all four perform the movements of the one who is speaking at a particular moment. In this
way the whole discussion takes on its own ritual and visual shape
and underlines the act of having to demonstrate the act of listening
in an existential way: everybody is over-sincere, and over-intel-
lectual and none of the dialogue is linked as discussion. SUPER-
MAN's naive and 'genuine' contributions are accompanied by mono-
lithic immobility: the others stop absolutely still to listen when he
speaks.)

CHORUS: All this in strange contrast to our famed hero. At the very same moment in time that the kids are screaming for Rock'n' Rollsen, Superman conducts a super-chore for charity.

CHAIRMAN: It is 2.25 and Superman speaks to you on the programme 'Inter-Facial-Arts-Confrontation'.

SUPERMAN: Another super-fee for charity.

CHAIRMAN: Ladies and gentlemen, the popular music business, records and public appearances, is a multi-million dollar proposition and yet the message it sells to young people implies a distinctly different way of looking at the world from that which is held by their parents or by the owners of the record companies. The economic momentum of the medium confounds old Marxian analysis. And this afternoon we are pleased to have with us that well-known music critic from the Daily Planet, Con Geel.

CON GEEL: Well, now, it's really great, just to, er, and to have, er, the opportunity of, er, I feel...

CHAIRMAN: Thank you Con. Also writing for the same newspaper, Phyllis Milchbrunchburger.

PHYLLIS: Well, hello, hello, hello.

CHAIRMAN: Thank you Phyllis. And from London, England, that well-known gossip-columnist, Angela Royston-Smythe.

ANGELA: Oh, hello my darling.

CHAIRMAN: And as our guest of honour for today... the one and only ... Superman!

SUPERMAN: Well hi.

ALL: Wow!

CHAIRMAN: 'The twelve-inch long-playing vinylite phonograph record with its half an hour to forty-five minutes of songs is an intellectual time bomb'... and I quote. Your comments on that... Con Geel.

CON GEEL: Yeah, well, now, if you get right down, or to be more specific; if you don't get right down, or up for that matter, but if you get right into, or more precisely, with, or, in the idiom of the young people themselves, if you get right down to the real or nitty-gritty... then you find, or not so much find...

CHAIRMAN: Thank you Con... Phyllis?

PHYLLIS: Forms and rhythms in music are never changed without producing the most important changes in political ways and forms. The new style insinuates itself into manners and customs and from there it issues a greater force, goes on to attack laws and institutions displaying the utmost impudence until it ends by overthrowing everything both public and private.

CHAIRMAN: Both public and private...Superman.

SUPERMAN: Well...personally I like to see the kids enjoy themselves.

ALL: Wow!

CHAIRMAN (profoundly): The kids enjoy themselves, says Superman ...Con Geel...

CON GEEL: Yeah, well now. This is exactly the point, or rather is exactly the opposite of the point, I was trying to make, or rather, tentatively to suggest, just a moment ago, or perhaps, earlier, which was that if you get down, up or into or with what the young people are doing or failing to do with their culture, or non-culture, or anti-culture, or rock culture...

CHAIRMAN: Thank you Con. Your thoughts on that now, Phyllis Milchbrunchburger.

PHYLLIS: Rock and roll uses Pavlovian techniques to provoke neuroses among its listeners.

CHAIRMAN: Angela Royston-Smythe?

ANGELA: Oh yes, oh yes, Pavlovian techniques, yes yes.

CHAIRMAN: Thank you Angela...Superman.

SUPERMAN: I mean to say...which one of you would like to stop the kids' enjoyment?

CHAIRMAN: Who indeed, Superman? And briefly...Con Geel.

CON GEEL: Yeah, well now. The important thing, or more specifically, the least important thing that needs to be remembered, or rather, is that if, that is rock'n'roll, is only nigger-music...

CHAIRMAN: Thank you Con...Phyllis?

PHYLLIS: It's only nigger-music!

CHAIRMAN: Now, finally, Angela Royston-Smythe.

ANGELA: Oh yes...it's only nigger-music.

(During these lines the other characters freeze in cartoon frame.)

CHORUS: So all is in apple-pie order in Metropolis. It would seem that nothing could disrupt this happy scene...or could it...

CHAIRMAN: And in summation...Superman...

SUPERMAN: Please! Let us remember these kids they're white, they're black, they're yellow, they're brown - they're AMERICAN and they have God on their side.

(At this point the discussion and patterns of movement break down, as the participants express their amazement and awe at SUPER - MAN's originality and then, repeating his phrase, discuss ani- matedly amongst themselves its implications until interrupted by a chord from the musicians which is the cue for the CHORUS.)

ALL: It's only nigger-music etc...

CHAIRMAN: What a mind, ladies and gentlemen... what more can one say...

CHORUS: Meanwhile, back at the theatre. Jimmy begins his act.

(As JIMMY performs the first verse SUPERMAN and the TV people freeze.

The SINGER sings while JIMMY mimes the first verse of 'High School Confidential'.

This is a fast rock song which is performed slowly in order to focus on some of the more ludicrous and grotesque aspects of the song itself, the style of singing and the style of movement of the early rock bands. In the final chorus the music inexorably builds up speed until only SUPERMAN is capable of dancing. He drops on the final chord.)

CHORUS: And amazingly, many miles away... Superman begins to rock and roll.

(SUPERMAN begins to jive, very expertly and dynamically with the CHAIRMAN while the SINGER sings the second verse.)

SUPERMAN: My super-hearing is picking up music from somewhere and it's making me dance... it's like the legendary flute of the Pied Piper.

(The other participants follow SUPERMAN as if he were the Pied Piper.

SINGER sings the third verse and repeats the chorus.)

LITTLE GIRL (saying her prayers):
What uncanny spell has affected the man of steel?
What can have caused our hero to lose control?

CHORUS (anxiously to audience): Unable to shut out the pounding rhythm, Superman has continued to jive until Jimmy's performance has ended as the coolest, while Superman's has ended in hot water.

(The above should be a genuine lament over a major catastrophe in the life of the city.)

SUPERMAN: My rock'n'roll really rocked the boat... everybody's hoppin... mad.

(The CHORUS turns away from SUPERMAN one by one as he tries to make a joke.)

CHORUS: Superman's fame as a rock and roller spreads fast!

(In the following sequence the GROUPIE strips, trying to get
through to SUPERMAN. She recalls the names of her conquests
(a more ritual Alice's Restaurant). The essential element of the
scene is the gradual build-up of the GROUPIE's vocal rhythm towards an orgasmic climax. Her words are repeated as many times
as is necessary or augmented with other names. It is accompanied
by counter-rhythms from the chorus. The chorus uses comic strip
words (ouff, gasp, owww etc.) which would be readily applied to
sex as a fairly crude pornographic function (slide, ride, astride,
slip, drip, grip etc.).

The GROUPIE's function is the temptation of SUPERMAN who is
assumed like Christ to have come by his moral beauty via spiritual
forces. He has apparently never lowered himself to actually ex-
periencing human emotions. The scene comes at a time when
SUPERMAN might be tempted to seek solace, after his humiliation
on TV.

The CHORUS's masturbatory rituals, though they are related in their
vocal rhythms to the GROUPIE's stripping, should appear to ignore
her and should be directed outwards at the audience...it is both
a meditation between the GROUPIE and the audience and also a
comment on the audience as they watch the 'exciting' dance before
them: it should deride the audience's experience by physically
mirroring their 'mental' processes.

After the climax the GROUPIE becomes inanimate at SUPERMAN's
feet and SUPERMAN examines her naively and intimately as if
she were a new and interesting object. The CHORUS retire exhausted, muttering appropriate obscenities. The GROUPIE comes
to life as SUPERMAN crawls to the piano and switches on the
musicians as if they were a gramophone record by beating the time
for the number on the piano. She does a rag-doll stripper's dance
which is overt and banal. By the end of the song she is inanimate
again. She is then dressed by SUPERMAN as the CHORUS sits
round them sniggering and jeering like nasty adolescents. As
SUPERMAN senses their presence his efforts to dress her become
more and more embarrassed and hurried. He is finally reduced to
demonstrating his strength in order to stop their smirking. They
stop but then recommence as his attention turns once more to the
problem. He retreats on the completion of his task with the CHORUS
openly laughing at him...he is obviously embarrassed and confused.)

GROUPIE:
   I've had it with Screamin' Jay Hawkins
   I've had it with Elvis Presley
   I've had it with Gene Vincent
   I've had it with Little Richard.

(The SINGER sings 'Breathless', originally sung by Jerry Lee

Lewis, as pornographically as the song suggests, as the GROUPIE strips.

The last verse is sung childishly to the accompaniment of the music box tinkling at the top of the piano.)

(The 'Earl' scene, which follows, may be played as a silent film with words, that is to say very quickly and with only a broad outline to suggest the action, much of which can be mimed or developed as any American crime series suggests itself. MONDAY is an obvious parody of Joe Friday of 'Dragnet'; the EARL the typical aristocratic melodrama villain; the HOODS a pair of imbecilic toughies from the Bronx; and the MOLL is the dumb blonde. Their movements are dictated by the era or convention chosen: they could be played in the 'realistic' manner with the reality of violence imposed on the scene in the way Hank Jansen might be treated on the stage; they are obviously two-dimension manifestations of violence and the mass delight in not sharing the pain of the pro-tagonists.)

MONDAY: July 16th - 2.19pm... Superman patrols above Metropolis City. Meanwhile in a downtown basement; English immigrant rackets baron, Anselm Dorsy, alias 'The Earl', conspires with his accomplices, Punchy de Witt and Bubu Jakulski and his moll, Vanda de Groin. Each is known to the C.C.R.O., Central Criminal Records Office, for unproved acts of 69/96f, 'granny-bashing'. The Earl is adding up significant clues from the daily newspaper.

EARLY: My jolly word, that blessed singer chappie performs each blinking afternoon at 2.30 and Superman makes a bally fool of him-self at exactly the same time.

HOODS: So what boss?

MONDAY (as one of the hoods): In actual fact, I am Joe Monday, F.B.I. under-cover agent, working incognito inside the criminals' gang.

EARL: Strike a light and stone the crows, old man. Don't you get the blimey point? After my spot o' tea and an innings of cricket, I'll tell you my A1 wheeze for copping a fearful lot of booty and not worry over that superchap's meddling, by jove.

(The gang assume a melodramatic plotting position.)

MONDAY: Planning his raid to coincide with Jerry Olsen's concert in the hope that Superman's strange dancing will let them escape un-harmed, the gang speed to the Georgetown intersection and their unsuspecting victim.

(The huddle becomes a car - aided by a kazoo or car noises off.)

At the same time, white-haired Dolores Schumacher, a 79-year-old widow, attempts to cross the road with her life savings, 18 dollars and 9 cents. She is planning to pay the first instalment on her spastic grand-daughter's pulmonectomy, a 62/27/13D transplant with lung.

(They get out of the car, which MONDAY parks, and walk to their positions - the GIRL engages SUPERMAN's attention; feels muscles, generally makes up to him - the plan is executed with apparently split-second timing.)

MONDAY: It is now 2.28pm, July 16th. The Earl positions his hoods and one of the darkest chapters in the history of American crime is about to be written. The plan: the Earl will leave Dolores Schumacher in the middle of the road to be knocked down by de Witt in the gang's 1957 Ford Eldorado. Jakulski will then shoot and rob her. They will escape by automobile.

(They execute their plan.)

2.29........their joy is short-lived. Superman has witnessed these heinous acts and races into action.

SUPERMAN: The Earl and his mob have knocked down and robbed that innocent old lady. I've been itching to get them...now's my chance!

(SUPERMAN stops the car with his superbreath...but he starts to dance and the gang get out of the car to mock.)

SUPERMAN: Oh no, it's that stupid music again...

EARL: Ha. Ha. Ha. We jolly well timed our act just when Rock'n' Rollsen started his jolly old act in Metropolis, by Jingo.

MOLL: Look at Superman doing his silly dance, letting us get away.

EARL: Pip, pip, superchap. Sorry we haven't got time to stay and watch your act. It's the giddy limit but we have some lucre to divvy up. Toodlepip, cheeriebye, keep your pecker up, old super-bean.

JAKULSKI: Jeepers...a super-boob by super-stoop. Haw, haw, haw.

MONDAY: At 2.30pm, July 16th, the fateful hour, Superman began to dance and the crooks escaped, laughing. None of these criminals has yet been caught. No names have been changed to protect the innocent nor hide Superman's guilty shame.

SUPERMAN: Boy, is my face red letting the crooks get away. If only I knew the answer to this riddle.

CHORUS (explaining to the audience): Jimmy Olsen, friend of Superman, is unaware that magnetic impulses from the concealed tape-recorder are being transmitted to Superman via the special wrist watch Jimmy uses to contact Superman in an emergency, and it is these specially powerful ultra-sonic impulses that have such a disastrous effect on Superman.

(The CHORUS circle round SUPERMAN and begin to sing a weird
and distant combination of harmonies – it grows in volume as they
move away from SUPERMAN who still sits confused centre stage.
As the volume increases he becomes increasingly more interested
and relaxed by the beauty of the sound.)

SUPERMAN: My super-hearing is picking up the sweet music of com-
munication from the furthest constellations. What can they want to
tell me?

(He begins to translate the music into words.)

Let there be light and there was light.
Let the earth bring forth the herb and the flower and the fruit.
Let the oceans and skies bring forth fish and fowl abundantly.
Let the earth bring forth man in his own image.
These things have inherited the earth.

(The harmony of the spheres is suddenly broken by a sharp and dissonant sound from the voices – it should occur like a warning.)

But - however - nevertheless - in spite of...

(The music is resumed, now full of dissonant menace and warning.
Tense and ominous, each voice communicates a different message
in different sounds. They should be obviously mechanical and distant, becoming increasingly urgent over the length of the sequence.)

Man is a polluted river...
Cruelty is the light of his soul...
The soul monstrous and deformed...
The body all lean and famished...
We are the prophets of the lightning and the heavy drops from the
    cloud.
Behold we give you this lightning...

(Having built to a climax on the last line, the music becomes even
more fragmented: isolated, random sounds, staccato and urgent,
spat out by the CHORUS.)

A great crack in the earth.
Severe unnatural weather conditions.
Electrical powers of great force.
Chaos in the movements of the planets.
Destruction of all...imminent.

(The fragmented sounds gradually come together to form this final
unanimous instruction.)

CHORUS: Superman move to action now!

(Repeated three times.

SUPERMAN gathers up his strength to meet the mighty task but is
halted by the SINGER's shouted introduction to the next song.)

SINGER (all lines are call and response and shouted back by the
  CHORUS):
  Give me an f...
  Give me a u...
  Give me a c...
  Give me a k...
  Give me a fuck...

  (Ad infinitum until it has built into a very fast rhythm. SUPERMAN
  begins to dance again.

  The SINGER sings the Jerry Lee Lewis hit song 'Great Balls of
  Fire'.

  There are paroxysms of complete hysteria as the first act concludes.)

If it is necessary for an interval, this is the most convenient point.
The second half then begins with the following rhythm and blues, pointing
to the reactions and indifference of the people of the city and probably
the audience to the dilemma of Superman: something which refers to
the entertainments industry, a high kicking routine, or the song itself
could be sung as we did with a mimed parody of Paul Robeson as a
'minstrel'. ('Were You There When they Crucified My Lord' fits.)

SINGER:
  I hear them shouting and railing
  Sobbing and wailing... their accusations
  Against the man of steel
  Who is the cause they feel... of their tribulations:
  He'll get no pity
  Neither from the city
  Nor from the nations.

  Man of steel, man of steel,
  You'll be no friend of mine
  How will you face
  The shame and disgrace
  That you won by stepping out of line.

  The city's angry voice strikes deadly as a public curse
  And Superman is powerless to pacify the wounds they nurse.
  There's danger to face, and they fear lest bad gives place to worse.

  Man of steel, man of steel,
  We now have cause to doubt you.
  Wasn't it you who kept us alive?

Will Metropolis survive
Without you?

(CHORUS commence 'Jump down, turn around, pick a bale of cotton'
work routine, over which the SINGER explains that this is an ad-
vertisement to promote 'Coon-Fresh, the deodorant for coloured
people'.

Two white men and the MINSTREL perform this rhythmically in a
very fast-moving tight circle which is very controlled and very
violent. The one who is speaking moves forward, the others backward.)

FIRST WHITEY: Ya white motherfucker... I'm gonna kill ya.

SECOND WHITEY: Kiss ma ass, ya jive motherfucker.

FIRST WHITEY: Ah's gonna cut ya up and down.

SECOND WHITEY: Ah's gonna cut ya side to side.

FIRST WHITEY: Ahm gonna fuck you up so bad even ya momma won't
know ya.

SECOND WHITEY: White motherfucker, I don't play that shit... just
you wait...

FIRST WHITEY: Let me go, whitey, so I can kill ya.

SECOND WHITEY: Whitey, just you wait till I get my knife right up
your ass...

(SUPERMAN's introduction of the idea of brothers which is intended
to end the violence, gives rise to collective brotherly violence
against the NIGGER. He starts off with the 'right idea' but like in
all dreams his ability to control it is restricted by the overall
factor: where there is music or rhythm he gets caught up. As the
play progresses it confirms PHYLLIS MILCHBRUNCHBURGER's
remarks in the TV sequence. SUPERMAN progresses frustratedly
towards anarchy as his ability to affect the society he lives in
diminishes.)

SUPERMAN: Brothers!

FIRST WHITEY: What you say man?

SUPERMAN: Brothers.

BOTH: Huh?

SUPERMAN: Brothers.

SECOND WHITEY: Ya mean ya think him and me is brothers?

SUPERMAN: Brothers.

FIRST WHITEY: If we's brothers man...

SECOND WHITEY: Yeah...then...

SUPERMAN: On this happy scene we leave this commercial to promote 'inter-racial harmony'. Thank you all and goodnight.

(The scene recommences for real and the 'NIGGER', after dispensing with the white girl who has become the centre of his attention during SUPERMAN's conclusion, destroys his incensed white co-actors with a few well-trained karate blows.)

NIGGER: Whitey problem...whitey unrest...whitey demands...whitey population...whitey period...are becoming a threat...to our national security...ah'm tired of having...to deal with you diplomatically...and you're reaching the point...in numbers and degree of...your dissatisfaction...and the nature of your protests ...that it's apparent...you're tired of dealing with us...diplomatically...and I might also add...non-violently.

Now there's still a whole lot of use we can get out of whiteys. But we don't need so many of them...specially if we can't control them. With automation we can get through with about two...three million working whiteys and most of them would be entertainers.

(The crowd rise and resume their jigging rhythm again.)

Too many whiteys constitute a danger to our national security.

(The following street calls are accompanied by repeated 'news-boy' shouts in rhythmic chorus.)

CHORUS:
Read all about it...
In the Daily Planet...
Read all about it...

FIRST CHORUS SPEAKER:
Superman blows cool on TV.
In the Daily Planet...

SECOND CHORUS SPEAKER:
Superman ignores Earl's monster crime
Read all about it...

THIRD CHORUS SPEAKER:
Superman cracks up over global crisis.
In the Daily Planet...

FOURTH CHORUS SPEAKER:
Superman gropes groupie.
In the Daily Planet!

(The CHORUS discuss the scandals animatedly with mounting indignation until one steps forward out of the crowd and speaks.)

The people of Metropolis demand an explanation

The people of America demand an explanation
The President of the United States demands an explanation
That afternoon on television Superman speaks...

SUPERMAN: The greatest thing I have ever experienced is this hour of the greatest...

(The next song which interrupts SUPERMAN's profound address to the nation turns into an anarchic attack on the values of the state. It is, however, communicated as if it were a brassy American TV show; with SUPERMAN as the star and three dancers whose overtly tough movements suggest both the song and the banality of the situation. Each time as SUPERMAN attempts to deliver his address and is interrupted by the music he becomes increasingly irate. SUPERMAN's words replace those of the song; his anger focusses on the audience.)

SUPERMAN: The greatest thing I have experienced is this hour of the greatest CONTEMPT.

(This is repeated three times – each time SUPERMAN attempting to regain his composure until he loses control.)

This contempt of the poverty
This contempt of the dirt
And the miserable ease
Of your decadent city.
What good is your virtue?
I am tired of you all,
Of your pathetic good and your pathetic evil.
What good is your justice?
I am sick of your laws
Of your petty restrictions.
What good is your pity?
What you should pity is your own mediocrity.
Have you ever spoken thus?
Have you ever cried thus?
Have you? Have you FUCK!

(CHORUS become Indians and sit cross-legged round SUPERMAN who becomes a totem pole in centre of stage. Making the various mystical Indian acknowledgements of greeting, they become silent until the CHIEF OF CHIEFS speaks.)

INDIANS (in rotation): How...

CHIEF: Running Deer speak.

RUNNING DEER: Big crack in earth... heap big evil... lose whole herd of buffalo down crevice.

CHIEF: Plenty storm brewing. Thundercloud over high mountain stampede war horses.

BRAVE: Sky spit down fire out of cloud. Awaken spirits of ancestors.

FIRST SQUAW: Silver maiden of evening and golden warrior of morning war in the heavens.

SECOND SQUAW: Voices from happy hunting ground speak...tell stories of broken arrow and blood river...squawling squaws and toppling tepees.

ALL: Oh, oh, oh, oh, oh, oh, oh, oh, wrath of great white father. Metropolis is evil. The city is possessed.

(One taking up the last words becomes a demonic baptist minister, working the CHORUS into a frenzy of fear and hate. The SPEAKER repeats the same two phrases with increasing dementia until the CHORUS are exhausted with the effort and lie under the seats or in the laps of the audience.)

SPEAKER: Metropolis is evil...

CHORUS: Metropolis is evil...

SPEAKER: The city is possessed...

CHORUS: The city is possessed...

(SUPERMAN comes out of his totem stance and Frankenstein-like makes his prophecy - borrowed for the occasion from Ezekiel.)

SUPERMAN:
Howl ye!
Woe worth the days.
A sword shall fall on Metropolis
And great pain shall be upon the city
And it shall take away her foundations
And Metropolis shall be in the midst of the country that is desolate
And the city shall be wasted
And you will know that I am Superman
I, Superman, have spoken it.

(The news flash sequence begins abruptly with HIRAM HOUSEBOAT jumping up and speaking into a microphone. Whilst each reporter communicates the story, the CHORUS enacts the event as if it were a live occurrence being reported on the spot. The events should be violent like a cartoon - the news has no more effect that a cartoon. SUPERMAN is seen to be industrious in his support of the activities.)

HIRAM: Hiram Houseboat, NBC news.

CHORUS: Newsflash.

HIRAM: Superman's 'Have a Fuck on a Public Highway' Campaign was officially opened by Superman at midnight on the steps of the church of the Blessed Virgin of Metropolis. After a few brief ob-scenities, he went through 1,027 high school girls who lined the route from the church.

RANDY S: Christ, he's all prick!

HIRAM: ...said Randy Smallbore, the mayor's daughter who, by shifting her place in the line contrived to get fucked by Superman no less than thirty-four times.

MAYOR: I have asked the police department to turn a blind eye to this mild display of high spirits.

HIRAM: ...the mayor told me this morning...

MAYOR: After all, we were all young once.

HIRAM: So keep fucking you super sonofabitch.

ALL: Newsflash!

WARTY G: Warty Gooseflesh, PUS news.

ALL: Newsflash.

WARTY: A nationwide conspiracy by people with physical impurities was revealed by Senator Meccano today...

SENATOR: It is my belief that there are warts and moles in very high places...both in the mayor's office and in the White House.

WARTY: ...said the Senator at a press conference in Metropolis.

SENATOR: I will not rest until they are put down...in fact I will not rest until everyone is put down.

BOOGIE B: Boogie Badear, ROT news.

CHORUS: Newsflash.

(Everyone freezes except SUPERMAN and JIMMY.)

SUPERMAN: So you're Rock'n'Rollsen; you play that music the same kind that gets me into trouble...but of course there's no connection.

BOOGIE: Today was a good day for souvenir hunters as Rock'n'Rollsen wound up his series of concerts in Metropolis. Far-sighted fans who provided themselves with machetes and meat cleavers went home with quite sizeable portions of his body....

(Fans start hacking.)

FIRST FAN: I got his left leg from the knee down.

BOOGIE: Said one satisfied customer...others weren't so lucky...

SECOND FAN: I got his prick...but it's very small.

(They freeze.)

SUPERMAN: Hey, Jerry, what happened? Wait a minute, beneath that disguise...it's...it's Jimmy.

JIMMY: Yes, Superman. That last mob of souvenir hunters got me before I could finish my act... I'm lucky to be alive, I can tell you.

(SUPERMAN dismembers JIMMY calmly and brutally during his speech.)

SUPERMAN: I see, Jimmy. It all becomes clear to me now. Your Superman signal-watch sent out signals to my super-hearing and they made me dance. A pity the fans stopped you finishing your act...

GAPING L: Gaping Loosebowels. CLAP news...

ALL (sinking to the floor and crawling towards the audience): Newsflash!

GAPING: Simultaneous outbreaks of typhoid, dysentery, syphilis and bubonic plague are reported from all parts of the city. To avoid further congestion of subways and elevators, sufferers from any of these complaints are advised to slip quietly into their nearest sewer for immediate disposal.

(The CHORUS rise and make the following announcement.)

CHORUS: And now for our final programme we go over to Superman who has just ferreted out the last remaining pockets of decency and incorruption in Metropolis... see him tell it to them like it is!

(SUPERMAN demonstrates the easy art of injecting drugs into the arm. The CLASS follow his movements with the naivety of a junior art class. They manifest the effect by all whispering intently wow! The ritual is simplified and accelerated and then brought down to its crude and terrifying ritual simplicity.

This call and response pattern is intensified by SUPERMAN as he speeds up the ritual to a climax.)

SUPERMAN: Here amphetamine.

CLASS: Amphetamine.

SUPERMAN: Here morphine.

CLASS: Morphine.

SUPERMAN: Here methedrine.

CLASS: Methedrine.

SUPERMAN: Here demerol.

CLASS: Demerol.

SUPERMAN: Here seconal.

CLASS: Seconal.

SUPERMAN: Here cocaine.

CLASS: Cocaine.

SUPERMAN: Here heroin.

CLASS: Heroin.

(The pace slows to slow motion and the CLASS reflect their withdrawal agonies through their physical and vocal contortions.)

SUPERMAN: Cocaine.

CLASS: Cocaine.

SUPERMAN: Heroin.

CLASS: Cocaine.

SUPERMAN: Here coke, coke, coke, coke...

CLASS: We want junk, junk, junk...

(As SUPERMAN begins to speak, the junkies' deprived moaning and snivelling changes into quiet demented laughter... conveying the madness of their condition.)

SUPERMAN (dancing a jig rhythm):
What I see must be... now
To was or not to have been
In the middle of nineteen hundred and yesterday....
What that is
What that ain't .... now
What that could be
Before it ain't it was
Yesterday is coming back tomorrow.

(SUPERMAN, with a powerful blow, destroys the laughers one by one... zap, pow, zowee, bam etc. They sink very slowly to the floor. SUPERMAN thrusts the needle into his body trying to kill himself.)

SUPERMAN:
What will the everlasting man do without the comfort of death?
Behold I give you the Superman
Behold I give you the deathslayer.

(The musicians begin a slow insistent rhythm which the actors join one by one with strange noises, kazoos, whistles etc. as the rhythm reaches a crescendo. It gradually becomes dissonant and unbearable, both in volume and pitch: it should sound like the chaos of the end. SUPERMAN sits on the floor doing his physical jerks in time to the music. As it breaks down his exercises get stranger and wilder until the music ends and the lights go out.)